An Insider's Guide to Property Development and Investment

BY JOHN HOWARD

Copyright © 2021 John Howard

ISBN 978-1-80049-572-2

This book is sold subject to the condition that it shall not, by way of trade or otherwise, be lent, resold, hired out, or otherwise circulated without the publisher's prior consent in any form of binding or cover other than that in which it is published and without a similar condition, including this condition, being imposed on the subsequent purchaser.

CONTENTS

About the Author — vii

Acknowledgements — ix

Chapter 1 – Getting Started — 1

Chapter 2 – What to Buy? — 5

Chapter 3 – What Type of Developer Are You? — 7

Chapter 4 – Personal Experience and Personality — 9

Chapter 5 – Timing and Intuition — 11

Chapter 6 – Money Matters — 13

Chapter 7 – Adding Value to Your Property — 15

Chapter 8 – Finding Deals — 19
- Estate Agents — 19
- Deal Finders — 21
- Property Auctions — 22
- Solicitors — 26
- Advertising — 26
- Social Media — 26
- Planning Portals — 27
- Associations and Clubs — 27
- Knocking on Doors — 28

Chapter 9 – Negotiating to Buy and Sell — 31
- Buying — 31
- Selling — 35

Chapter 10 – How Much is the Property Worth?	39
Chapter 11 – Negotiating the Sale Price	43
– Being in a Chain	45
– Price Reductions	46
Chapter 12 – Funding Deals	49
– Financial Backers	49
– Bank Funding	51
– Bridging Finance	52
– Personal Guarantees	53
– Building Societies	54
– Buy-to-let mortgages	55
– Private Loans	56
– Mortgage Broker	57
– Family	58
– Inheritance	59
Chapter 13 – Location	61
– University Cities	64
Chapter 14 – Choosing Tenants	67
Chapter 15 – Refurbishments	71
– Sales Tips for Renovations	73
Chapter 16 – Listed Buildings	77
Chapter 17 – Conservation Areas	79
Chapter 18 – Buildings with Enforcement Notices	81
Chapter 19 – Dealing with Builders and Other Tradesmen	83
Chapter 20 – Choosing a Solicitor and Estate Agent	89
– A Word of Warning	96

Chapter 21 – Buying and Selling at Auction	97
Chapter 22 – Residential or Commercial?	103
Chapter 23 – Houses or Flats	107
Chapter 24 – Purchasing New Builds Off Plan	113
Chapter 25 – Trading in a Hot Market	115
Chapter 26 – Trading in a Dropping Market	119
Chapter 27 – Accountants and Tax	123
Chapter 28 – Reducing the Agreed Price	125
Conclusion	131

ABOUT THE AUTHOR

John Howard is one of the most experienced property developers and investors in the UK today. During his 40-year career he has bought and sold approximately 4000 properties.

One of his most recent projects is a £27 million development of 150 apartments situated on the Ipswich Waterfront.

John was a major shareholder in Auction House UK, helping to make it one of the leading property auctioneers in the country. And this, alongside owning a number of estate agents, gives him a unique insight into the market.

His passion for advising and helping less experienced property developers and investors has led him to launching the John Howard Joint Venture Fund, where he co-invests with other property developers and offers his own guidance and mentorship.

Alongside numerous television appearances and speaking appearances and seminars, John is the executive producer for two shows on Property TV, namely Property Elevator and the Property Graduate.

ACKNOWLEDGEMENTS

This book certainly wouldn't been written without the help of my mother, Betty, who on my 18th birthday lent me the deposit for my first property deal. She showed great confidence in me, and I shall be eternally grateful to her for that. Thankfully, she also made a good profit!

My bank manager at the time also deserves a mention for lending me most of the money; it certainly wouldn't happen if I were starting my career now.

And to the agents, deal finders and others who over the years I have traded with, bought from, and sold to, I offer my thanks.

I would also like to acknowledge my long-term financial backers who have stuck with me, when I phone up and say 'this is one we should be buying', and usually doing so without hesitation.

CHAPTER 1
GETTING STARTED

I believe in keeping all elements of our lives as simple as we can, and this is a mantra that I certainly apply to dealing in property. Whether you are considering investing or trading, it is a simple business, and to forget this can come at the cost of your sanity and potential profits. And for this reason, I would recommend avoiding becoming too cerebral in your property dealings. Don't overthink a deal. Don't overanalyse a deal. You need to be able to get off the starting blocks.

If you are new to property developing, start at the beginning and evaluate your options. Some questions I would recommend asking yourself:

- What do you want to do?
- How much risk do you want to take?
- How quickly would you want a return on your investment?
- How much money do you want to make?

It is, naturally, advantageous to have another income alongside property. Whether this is full-time or part-time to subsidise your property dealings, but this isn't to say it cannot be done on limited funds. Although, being able to fund your living costs away from the property proceeds, even in the beginning, means you are able to reinvest these. Reinvesting your profits, is advantageous from a tax perspective, but also allows you to reinvest theme into your next deal, meaning you can grow your portfolio or do bigger deals.

However, some of you will want to focus full-time on your property business, like I do, and as such you need to be highly active. You need to network and get to know people, especially those who will buy you off, whether it's before you have paid for those properties or straight away afterwards. You just be able to find, buy and sell properties very quickly in order to make a living and to keep the money turning over.

This leads me to another option, becoming a deal finder for others with a full-time job. Some people don't have time to find the deals, and so rely on others to do it for them. Becoming a deal finder can be your only role, you can do this alongside your job, or alongside your own investments. Because not only do some people not have the time to source deals, you also are unlikely to be able to do every deal you come across and will still be paid a finder's fee for introducing the deal to someone else.

You may also be able to manage other properties for them or oversee building works prior to the sale or lease of a property. Potentially even turning your own hand to decorating or more general building work, using this to raise the necessary funds to purchase your own properties.

It is up to your individual situation which of the above ways of getting involved in property will work best for you, or which combination works.

There is an old anecdote of a cleaner who every night emptied the wastepaper baskets at a bank after everyone had gone home for the day. From here, she began absorbing the information and eventually was able to work out which shares to be investing in. Starting with a small portfolio and growing it from there whilst continuing to work on cleaning the bank at night.

Essentially, the lesson here, is that even the nation's biggest property developers began somewhere, normally this was by building or renovating just one property. Just make sure your first deal is a good one and remember that cleaner that never became too important to empty the bins.

CHAPTER 2
WHAT TO BUY?

There are of course some universal principles for property dealings but deciding what type of property you want to buy might be about the most important issue, and this is completely individual for you.

Deciding what to buy should be primarily motivated by what is of interest to you personally. There is very little point in doing a job that you aren't suited to and doesn't interest you. I can guarantee that this won't lead to long term satisfaction. And secondly, you need to consider your own financial situation, and how much you can afford to invest to begin with.

Both of these factors are subject to change throughout the course of your journey, and I recommend periodically sitting down with yourself and asking yourself these same questions. Additionally, after a few projects you may find that you have really enjoyed a particular deal and start to specialise in this area. Once your connections start to know what your specialisms are, they will automatically contact you when similar deals arise.

I cannot emphasise enough the importance of choosing property that inspires you. Whether this is buying houses in needed of renovation or building up a rental portfolio of commercial or domestic properties, all are a good choice if they suit you. The challenge you will encounter, is not finding these properties you are passionate about, but finding them at the right price so that you can make a good profit.

I found myself most enjoying projects that involve flats. This has been mainly conversions, and more recently I have been doing problem sites, particularly those without planning permission. Partially because I have often been able to sort out the problems and having been doing this for some time, I have built up a relationship with banks and as such they will lend me money on sites with no planning, knowing that I can sort this out and sell it on for a profit.

CHAPTER 3
WHAT TYPE OF DEVELOPER ARE YOU?

I have seen many builders move into property developing, believing they have 'seen the light', they want to make the money for themselves, rather than others by building the houses themselves. The problem here, is that often, these builders are craftsmen and are in danger of building the house too well. I would like to clarify here that I don't mean developers should be cutting corners with shoddy workmanship, rather than building to a very high specification than is needed means that prices need to be set higher than what buyers are willing to pay for similar properties. A more sensible approach is to build the property to a specification that allows you to sell at a competitive price, giving you the profits sooner and being able to invest these into the next deal.

Estate agents also often take up property developing themselves after having worked for an estate agency chain or an independent local agent. Having learned their craft on the front line many estate agents make very good property developers, providing they don't believe their own hype! Those who do become a little braver and break out of their employed status soon realise there is a lot more money in buying and selling than there is in taking calls and showing interested purchasers around houses on their company's books.

CHAPTER 4
PERSONAL EXPERIENCE AND PERSONALITY

When people think of property developers, I know the stereotypes of gregarious, loud, and risk-taking individual, but the truth is often rather different, particularly when we consider those who have been successful.

Those who are cautious in nature often make very good property developers, providing they are not entirely risk averse and still possess the confidence to take the plunge when the time and price is right. Being cautious can be a great quality to possess as a property developer, especially if you are able to establish an exit strategy for the eventuality when things don't go to plan.

Being a great property developer is all about finding the middle ground between confidence and cautiousness. Being over-cautious could result in you never buying anything, as it's very easy to talk yourself out of a deal. What I recommend if you are this person, is to ask yourself, 'what happens if things don't go to plan?', if the answer to that question is feasible and acceptable, then do the deal.

On the other there are those of us who are over-confident, and in this case, you still need to be making sure that your plans will not be too adversely affected if things don't go to plan. However, if you balance this confidence with realism, then you have a recipe for success.

It is also worth iterating that if you have any experience in a field that can be used to your advantage for property development, clearly you should be utilising this. And sometimes you will find that these skills can be used to lower your overall costs. n

CHAPTER 5
TIMING AND INTUITION

It is often said that the most dangerous time for a new developer is the third deal. The first deal, you are likely to be very cautious and take a great deal of time to mull things over and put in significant effort to ensure you get it right. For the second deal, you will probably take less time to think it over and anticipate that you'll be okay, but still it is only your second deal, so you haven't yet developed that gung-ho attitude. The third deal, however, can sometimes become a complete mess as over-confidence begins to creep in. New developers may pay too much, develop an ego, or believe too much of what they have heard from others. And for this, I just remind you; if it were that easy, everyone would be doing it (and succeeding)!

Of course, in a very 'hot' market (almost) anyone can do it, because you can rely on inflation alone. In this kind of market, you need minimal skill but there is still some need for intuition and common sense. However, it is getting out of this 'hot' market at the right time where the experience and knowledge will show, but few people do this because of greed and a fear of not being 'in' the market.

An astute property developer will prefer a market that is flat or in recession, because there is far less competition and far more opportunities, and therefore more chances to make more money.

It requires a huge amount of bravery to sell up your whole portfolio, or a significant amount, and wait for the market to drop, even when you know that market has got to drop at some time. Additionally, taxation, of course, plays a role, because if you sell up and have a huge tax bill, you will have less capital to invest even though the market has dropped. But you must remember in this case, you still have more than the person who went bankrupt.

Of course, if you haven't already borrowed too much, you can always be patient and wait for the market to return to its pre-recession levels.

Let's for a moment, think of the property market as a huge ship, it will take time to slow down, stop and then turn around. Sometimes you may be better to forget about the whole market for a year or two. Although, if you are like many other property developers, me included, you are a 'deal junkie' and always looking for the next big opportunity. But, with some good intuition and a little common sense, you'll find the deals that are there if there is one to be had.

CHAPTER 6
MONEY MATTERS

After deciding what type of property, you would like to buy and where your interests lie, you need to turn your thoughts to the logistics of this. You need to work out how much you want to be making out of your first deal and how much you should be paying for a property.

Traditionally, working to a net profit of 30 per cent after you have taken all costs and potential costs into account, including interest, was always the norm. However, you will probably have seen some TV shows that have perpetuated the idea that you can do a house up for pittance, and sell it on for a fortune, and I must tell you that the reality can be quite different.

In recent years, I have often been forced to work on a net profit margin of a minimum of 20%, this takes into account all expenses including solicitors, bank interest and building costs. You must account for all of these costs, to not do so is foolhardy and will only lead to disappointment. If you aim for a 20 per cent profit margin, you may in fact do better and consider this a bonus, but if you do worse then you still shouldn't lose money.

I'm often asked whether, as a property developer, a limit should be set on what to pay for a given property, and if so, how do I arrive at the correct figure to do so?

When dealing with a private treaty sale, the price is generally negotiable. When going through an estate agent you have the luxury of time to investigate prices, do your calculations and ensure that you offer the right amount of money. It is often said that the right price is the amount of money a buyer is willing to pay, so there is never going to be an exact and fixed amount of money. As a buyer you have the ability to negotiate and change what you have offered should circumstances change or problems arise. The vendor also has the right to accept or decline your offer.

When you are attempting to calculate your offer price, or at least the ceiling of what you could offer, remember the rule of making a minimum of 20 per cent net profit after all costs.

Should you like a property, and be able to envision yourself living there, you are likely to be far more biased about what you think it's worth, than if you don't see it as a potential home. So, you must put your personal feelings aside, and try and view the property from a prospective buyer's perspective. In order to ensure you only pay the true value of the property from an investment point of view, you must remain objective and remember whether or not you personally like the property is immaterial.

Furthermore, you should always be prepared to walk away, should the figures not quite stack up. If your assessment of the costs leads you to believe that you're not going to make the net profit you need to make as a minimum, then it's not a good deal. Additionally, never assume that you can cut costs based on the quote given to you by a builder, in my experience it almost always costs more than originally quoted.

CHAPTER 7
ADDING VALUE TO YOUR PROPERTY

In order to work out whether you are able to make a reasonable profit, you need to work out the costs, but you also have the opportunity to add value. When I am viewing a property for sale, I am always considering how I can add extra value to a property, over and above refurbishment or renovation. This can add to your bottom line dramatically.

For instance, if there isn't a car space in the front garden, you could potentially add £20,000 or more to a property. You may need permission from the council to put it a drop curb, and the council will probably have a list of contractors who are allowed to carry out this type of work and your builder probably won't be on this. It will of course come at a small cost but will far more than pay for itself.

If there is room to build a garage, consider this carefully. A brick-built garage will cost a lot of money, and people don't tend to look after their cars in the same way they used to, they are now a necessity to get you from A to B. As a general rule, a garage will not add enough value to make it worth you constructing this. However, a carport is an attractive and cost-effective way to add value to your property.

If the neighbouring property looks to be in terrible condition, this can certainly have an effect on the price you can expect to achieve for your property. An example could be, the house next door needs painting, and it may sound odd, but consider offering to paint the front of their house. Doing this could well make your house more saleable. Generally, the neighbours will be happy to accept your offer if it is delivered in the right way, and it benefits you too, whether it allows you to achieve a slightly higher price or just to receive your profits sooner.

The same can be said for if you buy a property and the neighbour turns out to be a hoarder. Some years ago, I bought a house next to someone who could never throw anything away, and this included rubbish that was piled in the front and back gardens. This can be a very serious problem, and it is not as simple as offering them a fresh coat of paint. I would advise you stay away from buying this house and let someone else deal with the problem.

Of course, the same can be said for a variety of issues with your neighbours, and you need to consider whether they are simply less house proud than the ideal neighbour, or whether their behaviour is truly antisocial. There are no guarantees once you have bought the property, you can't control someone else's behaviour, so as a rule I would tend not to purchase the property. I prefer to be in control of my own destiny.

And whilst I am on the subject, remember that the outside of the house is important too. When planning your costs, factor in enough to be able to tidy the front and back garden. You don't need to plan an award-winning piece of landscaping, but perhaps consider having a tidy lawn, or putting up a new six-foot fence.

Another option can be purchasing a little additional garden space from your next-door neighbour which will certainly increase the value of your house. This is called 'marriage value', but don't get carried away and spend £30,000 to buy a postage stamp of extra garden. I would recommend speaking with an agent as you need to ensure that after the purchase price, and the conveyancing costs for the extra land, you are still left with a profit from doing this, as in some cases it can even lose you money.

Attics also can get people quite excited. Firstly, you need to check the head height in the roof, and if you can make a genuine room without massive expense then you can add an extra bedroom or office. But still, do your research, check with your trusted agent, because the cost can be more than the return you may expect.

I will mention cellars later in the book, but if you do visit a house with a cellar, you should be aware that it is very expensive to bring these into domestic use, even when they have windows. My advice with cellars is leave them alone, except from in exceptional circumstances. In fact, an inexperienced buyer may even see this cellar and hopefully they will think that you have missed a trick by not already converting this.

Remembering these things will help you when selling, but also are important to remember when you are viewing properties. If a house has problems, it can be a great opportunity to make a great profit, but it can also be a sign to stay away, and you must learn the difference.

CHAPTER 8
FINDING DEALS

As I mentioned earlier, you can find deals as your main source of income or do this alongside your own developments. And, like is often said, 'it's not what you know, it's who you know' and in this case, this is certainly true.

ESTATE AGENTS

There are numerous ways of finding deals, and the most obvious and old-fashioned is going to your local estate agent and asking what they've got on their books that fit your category of interest. In my experience, the odds of you finding a deal which can make you a 20 per cent net profit this way are slim, but not nil and as such it's worth getting to know your local agents.

In order to build a relationship with an estate agent you need to forge a mutually beneficial partnership. It may mean popping your head around the door every few weeks, eventually buying them a coffee and bringing this in with you – and remember the doughnuts! This makes them remember you and what you are looking for, and it can mean them looking forward to you coming in again.

This is a piece of advice that works with estate agents but can be applied to your relationships in the wider context; I use the notes app on my phone (and used to use a small notepad) to write down something memorable about my visits. This can be that an agent's wife is due to have a baby soon or that someone is going on holiday. So, next time I go back I have a conversation starter. Making connections with people will make it easier and more likely that you will do business with them.

You should be very clear about exactly what you want to buy, and make sure that you can clearly express this. If you are vague, they won't know whether to contact you or not. And if you can make this crystal clear, then you could be one of the first of fifty that they might ring. And, when they do call, get back to them straight away, responding and making decisions promptly ensures that you don't drop down to the bottom of their list.

If you feel it to be appropriate you can suggest there could be a drink in it for them personally, which is now an old-fashioned term, but means that if they find a deal which you chose to do you may give them something in return. These days we don't give money, but I may discreetly pay for them to go away for the weekend, letting the hotel know I'm covering the bill. However, in some cases now this isn't appropriate and can instead been considered a conflict of interest for the agent who should be acting on behalf of the seller.

On top of this, I always pay a company or a self-employed agent a two per cent finder's fee, and if I am refurbishing the property to resell then I automatically give it back to them to put on the market for me.

Over the years, I have rarely bought property which is currently on the market because someone is always prepared to pay more than I will. Generally, the properties I buy have either been on the market and not sold, or not yet gone on to the open market. I am able to do this because of the relationships I have built up with estate agents and other individuals who find deals.

It is worth me mentioning, that you have a much better chance for getting a good deal out of a lazy agent than one who is on the ball. Although ideally it is the second one that you need to be selling the property onwards for you.

DEAL FINDERS

I work with quite a lot of people who make a living off finding deals for developers. I have worked with one such person for twenty-five years now, and he often finds me deals, for which I pay him a fee. I also pay him a fee when we sell the properties, even if he is not involved.

Deal finders may also do their own details and have their own portfolio. So, like the rest of us, they can't buy everything, so if they find something that they aren't able to do on their own, they are normally very happy to pass it on for a fee. As you meet with more people and begin to network with other people trying to do the same thing more opportunities will come to you in this way.

I have dealt with numerous property consultants during my career and had different arrangements with each one. Some consultants have been on retainer, and we have paid them a monthly salary. However, paying a consultant like this when you are in the earlier part of your career probably won't be possible, but can be worth considering for when you are consistently purchasing properties.

And, I hate to say it, but a recurring theme is, that it's not what you know, but rather who you know.

PROPERTY AUCTIONS

Property auctions are another great way of buying and selling property and have undoubtedly become more popular in recent years. I am a former director of Auction House UK, and after we purchased the business in 2009 it grew from seven to 41 franchises, mainly because of people like yourselves who were looking to get into investing in property. And I must thank TV programmes like Homes Under the Hammer for this also, as they seemed to be filming at one auction or another around the country most weeks.

The great thing about buying and smelling at auction is that it is instant. When the hammer comes down on a winning bid, the buyer has bought the property and the seller has sold it, end of story. You then have 28 days to complete on the sale. As part of my strategy, I always try to have something for sale in the auction, as I know that money will then be coming in. Although, a sale on that particular day is not guaranteed.

It is really important that you always view a property prior to the auction. Many years ago, I stuck my hand up at an auction in London. I thought I had been very clever and managed to snag a shop and three flats in Liverpool for £5,500. At least I did until I viewed the property.

First, I went to see the tenant in the shop who informed me that he wasn't going to pay me any rent, because if he wasn't using it then it would need to be boarded up and I won't find anyone to let it to. As you can imagine, not a great start.

Then, I went to see the tenants in the flats above, and guess what? They also told me that they won't be paying rent because if they have to leave the flats will be vandalised. All in all, not a great start and I came away from Liverpool feeling rather deflated. That was until, I get a phone call from my solicitor, and deflated doesn't quite cut it. In the small print of the auction contract there was a clause which stated that I had to pay all of the rent arrears that were owed to the owners and attempt to claim this back from the tenants.

It was at this point that I decided to ring a friend, and and asked him to drive to Liverpool and replace a pane of glass in one of the flats that had been boarded up, as well as to repaint the front of the building and take a photograph. I then put the lot back in the auction, at the same reserve price and fortunately someone paid similar money. And, this may sound harsh of me, but my problem was now theirs.

I was lucky this time, you may not be so fortunate so please ensure you view the property prior to the auction.

Traditionally, you had to be very careful when buying at auction as there was normally a good reason why a property was being sold in one. For example, it could have subsidence and therefore be unmortgageable. Also, you need to check that the neighbouring buildings are being used for undesirable purchases and preventing you from being able to sell the property on. Auctioneers now have a legal responsibility to describe the property accurately in the catalogue.

The guide price, as stated in the catalogue, will be between two figures. For example, if it's between £50,000 and £65,000 then the reserve price is likely to be £57,500, although this is not always the case. Additionally, I would recommend checking with the auctioneer prior to the auction that the guide prices have not changed. It is also worth asking them what the reserve price of a particular property is, some will tell you and some won't, but it's worth asking.

As I said earlier, it's worth getting to know your estate agents, and the same is true for your local auctioneers. You'll find them to be very approachable, and they all have a big ego, something that's needed to stand on the rostrum, but this can be used to your advantage.

If you are thinking of bidding, then definitely introduce yourself before the auction starts and let them know that you will be bidding and like with your estate agents don't tell them the maximum you would be willing to pay. Not all auctioneers are as professional as Bryan Baxter of Auction House, one of the most experienced auctioneers in the UK. For example, Bryan stands on the rostrum well over 100 times a year, whereas some others may only do so a handful of times per year.

As I mentioned, the speed of the auction process is the thing I like the most about it, but modern advances are now making it more difficult to gain an advantage, such as all the legal packs now being available online. It's used to be that all the hard copies of the legal packs were left on a table. And, if there were a number of properties that you were interested in and bidding on, you could pick up the legal pack of a particular property and not return it until the auction was over, preventing anyone else from reading it. Sometimes they would announce, "whoever has the legal pack for lot number…please hand it back".

Even now, you'll be surprised how many people go to auction and haven't even read the legal pack prior to going, which as far as I'm concerned is their own fault. If you fail to plan, then you're planning to fail, it's as simple as that.

When I'm bidding at auction, I always set my limit and go no more than five per cent over it. This way, if I've only missed it by a small amount, I'm not kicking myself because I know I had already bid more than I should have. Set your maximum that you would like to pay for the property, and then allow yourself a five per cent buffer.

Don't panic if at the auction you are told the legal pack has been downloaded fifty times, and similarly don't get excited if it's only been downloaded by two. I have kicked myself plenty of times when I expected something to be very popular and find out it has sold for a lot less money than expected. Similarly, don't walk into the auction with certain expectations because the legal pack hasn't been viewed by dozens, as it only takes one person to be interested who is also prepared to pay more than you.

Another recommendation is that you have your lawyer glance over the legal pack, as well as having read it yourself. It never fails to amaze me how many people blind bid, meaning that they have not previously viewed the property or thoroughly examined the legals because they thought it was cheap on a given day. And, in most cases they have lived to regret this.

SOLICITORS

It used to be that solicitors were a great source of deals because they dealt with probate. This has since changed as they must advise their clients to use the normal routes for selling property, i.e., putting the property on the open market which will hopefully achieve the best price.

ADVERTISING

Another option is to put an advertisement in the local paper saying, 'property bought for cash'. And, particularly in tough times you'll be amazed how many calls you'll get. During the 2008 recession, I took this idea and added a modern spin, I had a website built called 'Properties for Cash', which for a while became quite successful.

SOCIAL MEDIA

I recently purchased a property in the very modern way, using Gumtree. I paid £45,000 for it and two months later I entered it into the next Auction House auction in Norwich, it sold that day for £78,000. I had done nothing to the property. Although I must say, these kind of deals are rare and become less and less common.

If you are computer literate, use the internet to your advantage. LinkedIn, Facebook and all of the other social media channels can now be used to your advantage. There are houses being sold and advertised all over the internet, so consider some of the more unusual and less traditional routes to making a profit. And, if you can't find what you're looking for on their, let people know what it is you want and get them to come to you.

It really is a case of nothing ventured, nothing gained, and all of these new sources are things that until now have been unavailable as part of the property developer's sourcing armoury.

PLANNING PORTALS

Another way you can find out about properties through the internet, is via the planning portal of each local authority. Everything is now in the public domain, including the addresses of proposed sites and all the property's drawings available for viewing. Normally there are even details of the owner or agent that are dealing with the matter, so it's a brilliant resource. You can then get in touch and find out if they want to do a deal.

ASSOCIATIONS AND CLUBS

Another excellent source of contacts is being a member of an investment club where you can become privy to a number of buy-to-let investments and other initiatives. Some of the property people who run these clubs have bought a number of houses or flats in bulk, normally at a large discount, and so can pass some of that discount on to you.

However, different associations work on different systems. Some don't buy any of the properties and work for commission from the developer, whereas others will purchase and resell. If you do consider buying some of these, make sure that you know what these flats or houses are actually selling for on the open market. Never blindly take the word of these investment clubs.

Landlord associations are another great way of networking and meeting like-minded people. This can be helpful for finding trusted tradesmen that other members have already been tried and tested, as well as keeping you up to date with relevant legislation.

KNOCKING ON DOORS

It isn't the first time in this book, and it won't be the last time you can accuse me of sounding old fashioned, but these methods are tried and tested, and have worked for me over the last forty years and continue to.

If you see a vacant house, or one that it is in particularly poor condition there is nothing wrong with seeing if you can find out who owns the house and if they are willing to sell. Always start by talking to the neighbours, as they normally tell you everything you need to know, without even thinking about it they will tell you all the information you are after.

If not, head over to the land registry website, and for a small fee you can do a search and find out who owns the property.

Remember that knowledge is power. If you can find out that the owner is short of money, or perhaps it's been left to someone who lives overseas and so the house isn't occupied and just deteriorating, then this might give them the needed incentive to want to make a deal with you on the house.

My final piece of advice on this topic comes from when I was training to become a qualified racehorse trainer. Toby Balding, the famous racehorse trainer to the Queen's horses came to speak to us, his advice; "never turn down a dinner party, you never know who you might meet". It is good advice whether you're looking to meet a racehorse trainer or financial backer, and you may even come across a new property deal!

CHAPTER 9
NEGOTIATING TO BUY AND SELL

BUYING

It is often said that a good outcome to any negotiation is one where both parties are happy and feel they have come away getting what they needed. Although, I'm not sure I agree with this, as successful negotiation for me is one where I'm happier than the other side.

As I said before, when you make an offer for a property make sure you keep you cards close to your chest and don't let the right hand know what the left is doing.

If an agent asks you what the most you're willing to pay is, tell them the offer that you've made is your ceiling. You'll be amazed how many people, when asked that question, will answer with their absolute maximum figure. Remember the agent is acting on behalf of the seller and as such, if they know that you will increase your offer, they will use this to your detriment.

Similarly, don't alienate the agent, or the seller, by offering such a low figure that it comes across as being insulting. Unless you have prior knowledge telling you that there is a chance that it will be successful, all it will do is irritate him and put his back up, so when you come to a sensible offer, they may hold on to their principles are refuse you regardless.

Whether the agent attains a few thousand more for the property, or not, makes almost no difference to his commission, but makes a huge difference to your profit margin. And, as such you need to make sure the agent is always on our side and we maintain a good relationship.

Let us assume that you're going to be buying a pretty standard house for renovation, here are some tips on how to get a great deal agreed.

If you have the money to purchase the property in cash (i.e., available funds, without any borrowing) then one of the easiest ways to get the property at the right price is to offer a very quick exchange and completion. To do this, you obviously need a solicitor who will work with you and is on your wavelength, but I will go into more detail on solicitors later.

Or the person selling the property might want to have more flexibility, something else you can offer. In other words, they might want the security or a very quick exchange, but the time afforded by a long completion to find their onward purchase. Again, this is something that you can work on with them in order to secure a great deal. You need to make the deal as easy and attractive for the vendor, this way they will sell to you and nobody else.

I always attempt to find out the very bottom price they would have accepted as a sale from the agent before I commit to any offer as it could actually be less than I was prepared to give as my first offer. Although, a decent agent shouldn't give this figure away, you may find that what they do tell you can be quite revealing. If you can get them to, let the other side commit first.

I also try to find out their situation when they are looking for a quick sale as knowledge truly is power. When you have this information, you can they use it to your advantage. Most people would be doing the same in your situation so don't feel embarrassed by this. It doesn't mean you are aggressive, unhelpful or unkind, in fact gaining rapport with the vendor is beneficial for both parties.

As I mentioned before, I bought a house directly through Gumtree. The owner was ill, and needed to sell desperately, and if he had held out for the highest bidder, he would not be afforded the time to enjoy and spend the proceeds from his sale. He wanted cash, and he wanted it quickly, and I was able to help him do this. To some, this may sound callous, but this was beneficial for him and for me, we both came away from the transaction having got what we need.

It may be that when you view a property you meet the owner rather than the agent. It used to be that agents would take you round every house, but this isn't always the case unless the property is vacant. There are certainly advantages to this. It provides you with a great opportunity to get on well with the vendor and find out what they are likely to take, and what they are likely to take and what their personal circumstances are. They should have far more knowledge about the property and what has or hasn't been done.

If you can meet the vendor directly, try to connect with him within the first minute of doing so. It may be that you both have a dog or a cat, or you walk in and see a photograph of their daughter in university robes. Whatever it is, find something and make that connection with them.

Furthermore, if during the negotiations you've hit a snag, but have already made a good impression and created a mutual respect, the vendor is far more likely to be flexible with you and prepared to work out a solution. It could be that you got overexcited and offered a little too much and now need to reduce the price in order for you to make you 20 per cent profit target from the deal.

It could be that you are just greedy and want to bid the price down just before exchange, and while this can work, it's not a strategy I would recommend. However, if you are going to employ this technique, send the 10 per cent deposit that you are exchanging with to the vendor's solicitors, so they know you mean business. I have had this done to me on numerous occasions, especially from other dealers. And, whilst it's never nice to be on the receiving end, it is business!

If you ever have the opportunity to achieve a delayed completion on any purchase, it's normally always good news. It can provide you with time to either sell the property on for more money, or if you plan to refurbish, then sometimes you can exchange contracts and get on and do some of the work. The sooner you can get the property back on the market, the better. The longer you hold on to the property, the longer you are paying interest. If they ask you for a larger deposit than normal on exchange of contracts, so that you can get access to do the work, this is still well worth doing.

If you are buying a property that someone has only just bought, before quickly selling it on don't let the price they paid influence you (should you find this information out). It doesn't matter how much profit they are making out of you, because this is effectively what you are trying to do to someone else when you sell that property on afterwards. If you are confident that you can make the profit that you want or require, that's all you need to know.

In the early 1990s I purchased two large tower blocks comprised of 280 flats in the West Midlands. I bought them off an Irishman who had acquired them six months earlier for £75,000 each. I paid him £1.5 million knowing what he had paid. I went on to make good money from these flats. Success lies in being confident in your own ability, and not concerning yourself with how much money someone else might be making as a biproduct of your endeavours.

In fact, if I am selling something straight on then I will tell someone else what I paid for the property. This way, it is all out in the open and they can make their own decision. This also protects you somewhat, you don't want them pulling out of the deal at a later stage because they find out what you paid and feel some type of way about this. I would rather know straight away if there were a problem, rather than wasting time on a deal that is going to fall through.

Additionally, with the internet and Land Registry, there is nothing you can't find out anymore, so being honest and straight to the point is the best policy.

SELLING

If you have refurbished a house, give it back to the agent you purchased the property from. This is really an unspoken agreement of 'honour amongst dealers and agents', and you need to hope that they are good at what they do. It can easily mess up a really good source of deals if they can't sell the property when you give it back to them to sell and later have to pass it to another agent.

I never try to negotiate the agents fee down too far. The reason for this, is that I want them to do a great job for me, and to sell mine before any others. Furthermore, I want to work with agents in the long term as it could be a very good source of deals in the long term.

If you have no loyalty to a particular agent, because you didn't buy this house from an agent, or perhaps it's in an area you haven't done a deal in before, to work out who the best agent is go on one of the property portals and see who has the most properties for sale. You will never see a successful mid-range estate agent with no properties to sell.

Steer away from dealing with young and inexperienced negotiators unless they're very special. Particularly if you are new to the game, you need an experienced agent on your side. Always go for the manager and don't get fobbed off. And bear in mind that at an agent is going to be on the optimistic side of what you can get. I often don't take their advice, but instead, I will put it on the market for less than what they say. To some people, this sounds counterintuitive, but everything I put on the market I want to sell within 28 days. The reason for this is because then I can move on to the next deal quicker. I'm not going to waste time pretending that a property is worth more, simply because I own it.

If you receive an offer within the first day or two, it isn't unreasonable for you to thank them for their offer but say you would like to consider other offers receive within the first week, before going to best and final. Don't just pick the person offering the most, pick the best buyer.

Hopefully, the best buyer is a cash buyer, and if they are then ensure your agent has received proof of funds and gauged how motivated they are to purchase. If there is more than one offeree, it is worth meeting them and seeing which buyer you sense is more serious, and which one you can trust and get along with. People can be unpredictable, but if you have a good sense for people this is worth taking the time to do. Your agent can also check them out, they may have done business with them before, or the agent selling their property may know them; they could have a reputation for offering on multiple properties or not proceeding with sales.

If circumstances allow, always help the agent out and allow them to put up a for sale sign. Don't concern yourself if they don't advertise in newspapers, in my opinion this is now one of the lease effective forms of advertising to get houses sold. Now, it's all about the online property portals, for example Rightmove or Zoopla, along with sites for more specialist properties – such as equestrianproperty.co.uk. Rather than doing print advertising, I would want to ensure that they will make your property available on all the major portals.

Online estate agents should be avoided. And especially please don't get sucked in by those that offer to sell your property for a modest upfront fee. An upfront fee ensures the agency has no incentive to actually sell the property and see this through to completion. More often than not, you will still end up having to use a traditional estate agent. This is not to say it cannot work in some circumstances, there are always exceptions, but you will only make money selling in this way when demand is particularly high, and supply is very low. I honestly believe that their business model is deeply flawed.

CHAPTER 10
HOW MUCH IS THE PROPERTY WORTH?

All estate agents are extremely optimistic, it is a prerequisite for their job. They also want to have your property on their books, and when you combine this objective with their nature, you find that a lot of them will overvalue your property in an effort to win your business. They will then spend the following months trying to work down the price to get it to a figure where it will sell, but you're a property dealer and so, for you, this is the completely wrong way to do it.

You may already have a relationship with the estate agent, they may have sold it to you in the first place, and if this is the case it won't come as a surprise to you when they tell you what they think you can sell it for, after they told you what you can expect for it when you first purchased the property.

Almost everyone who is selling a house asks for it to be put on the market for at least the money that it was valued for, if not more. But you must bear in mind that the initial valuation you had was optimistic, at the very least, and that's why I would say you should consider entering the marketplace below their valuation.

The most important time when selling a property is the first fortnight of it being on the market. If it's overpriced, you won't get the response you want, and by now you will have lost the impact and be forced to reduce it to what it should have been in the first place. Now, everyone has seen the property on the market, and it is stale.

Instead, what I would recommend and what I regularly do, is to put the property on the market at a slightly lower figure than the agent's recommendation. This makes the agent super keen to sell the property and you are far more likely to get multiple offers. And, if this happens, then normally you can get at least one party to increase their offer, this can go back and forth, so requesting the agent to instruct the offerees to go to best and final offers is a great strategy. During the time preceding the best and final offers, your agent should be doing their due diligence to ensure that what they have been told about the offerees circumstances is accurate.

At this point, I remind you that the best offer is not always the highest one. Remember that every day the property is yours, it is costing you money, and you are paying interest on the property. This lost time and money of a lengthy conveyancing process can rob you of the opportunity that could arise with another deal.

If you are getting frustrated that the property isn't selling, then it can be worth freshening things up by taking it off the market for a few weeks and returning to the market with a new agent at a further reduced price. I recommend reducing the price further, because you must give the new agent a chance to sell it and returning to the market at the same money is unlikely to have the impact you need to get it sold.

However, you should never put the property on with more than one agency. Signing a sole agency agreement is not a problem, but this should only be for a short period of time – four weeks will give them a sense of urgency. By going on the market with multiple agents you begin to look desperate, this only serves to cheapen your product. This may seem counterintuitive, as some believe that this gives some inter-agency competition, but I assure you this is not the case. You want your estate agent to be loyal to you and look out for your best interests when negotiating a sale, and for this to happen they need to like you and respect you – this motivates people to do their best for you.

Remember, don't be mean on the commission with your agent. Estate agents play a vital role in this business, it's a symbiotic relationship and as such you should pay them a decent commission. Between 1 and 2 percent is generally acceptable. Don't be too aggressive when negotiating commission, it's a false economy. Getting you agent on side gets them working harder for you, even if it is subconscious, the way that they conduct themselves towards potential purchasers will be impacted.

If you get a really low offer, then the buyer is probably taking liberties – and there are some who think they are being clever by doing this. In this case, stand up to them, politely decline the offer but keep a dialogue open, and continue to take the advice of the agent, that is what you are paying for. In this scenario, I would like to emphasise taking the advice of your agent. An agent will be less biased about the situation, and isn't too close to the matter at hand, agents will remain rational whereas when it is your own property it's harder to stay detached.

Never make a decision on the basis that you are angry about the amount. Take time to consider every offer and don't make any snap judgements, particularly as this could end up being your best offer in a reasonable time period.

CHAPTER 11
NEGOTIATING THE SALE PRICE

When selling the property, I recommend remembering and utilising the same tactics that you used to purchase. I am always amazed when a buyer tells an agent what their top offer would be, but then goes in at a lower figure. It's as if they forget that the agent works for the vendor, and it will be them that pay the agent's fees.

When the agent rings you to tell you they have received an offer, always ask if they know or have an indication of what the offeree will go to. This can save an awful lot of time and effort and can put you in a strong position for negotiations.

Ensure that an agent has checked out a buyer's financial position, whether this is that they are able to get the needed finance, can prove cash funds or that if there is a chain this is complete, and all parties are ready to proceed.

Another good idea is to check that a buyer hasn't been running around, making offers and wasting agents time. Although, I know this is not always possible, if they are in a chain and your agent speaks to their agent, they will often get a sense of how the offeree has been conducting themselves.

And remember, you don't have to respond to any offer immediately. Thank them for their offer, as the right questions and have a think about it - but don't take too long. Vendors have lost motivated buyers for taking waiting to decide.

Once a buyer has increased their offer to as much as the agent says they are willing or able to, and it's still not enough, try splitting it down the middle. For example, if you want £300,000 and they have offered £275,000 – see if you can get a deal agreed at £287,500. Another way to do this is to flip a coin for the difference, but this is something that few property dealers will do, let alone people buying the property to live in.

Throughout this book, I also want to remind you of the behaviours that I consider to be red flags. And one of these, is those who having immediately viewed the property want to buy it there and then – these people have normally made an impulsive decision, and often pull out. Additionally, if someone is taking too long to make a decision, for example needs a third viewing, I would be wary – these viewers are normally too busy looking for reasons why they shouldn't buy. And this is a good time to mention something else that I often tell people, if you have made an offer, normally people will be happy to entertain a third viewing, but until then you should have all you need to make a decision after two viewings.

For your agent, finding a buyer is just the start of their job, as 25% of offers will not reach completion. A lot of the best agents now have a sales progression team, whose role it is to see the process through to completion. It is important that both you and your buyer have good solicitors, as without their team being up to the task it will be far more difficult for your lawyer to see this through in a timely fashion.

Personally, to avoid being kept waiting too long, I always put by buyers on a 21-day exchange from receipt of the contracts sent from my solicitor. This timescale focuses both the buyer and their solicitor, telling them that we mean business. If this deadline isn't met, you can threaten to pull out and then give them an extended deadline – or if you're particularly brave you may want to ask for a price increase. How you handle the unmet deadline is down to you, but the most important part is that you are in control of the transaction.

BEING IN A CHAIN

If there is a chain behind your buyers it is essential that your agent has done their due diligence and inspected the chain to the best of their abilities, everyone must be in position to proceed. Speaking from personal experience, there is little that is more frustrating than having a motivated buyer who isn't able to because three links down the chain there is a problem.

Often you will have to accept that your sale is part of a team, all due for completion that same day. Naturally, the longer the chain, the greater the risk of the sale falling through. It is fairly common that one of the properties in the chain could be undervalued for their mortgage, and where this is happened, you can work towards persuading the rest of the chain to make small price adjustments to enable them to make up the difference and allow everyone to move on from this.

Once I have a good buyer, I will do everything I can to make sure the sale goes through. I have no pride or principles with regard to getting a sale through to completion. If you have one of these, often, you will cause the sale to fail when there's a problem.

PRICE REDUCTIONS

It never ceases to amaze me how often I am asked to reduce the price of a property, once the exchange of contracts draws near. Often this is because the survey hasn't come out quite as well as we would hope, or because the property has been down valued, or even that the buyer is just being difficult and thinks we need the money – which in a lot of cases, especially as a developer, you do to move on to doing your next deal.

On the whole I will agree to some renegotiation, having gone that far down the line the prospect of beginning the process a second time and that you may not even get the same money again is not a desirable prospect. Additionally, you can't move on to the next deal so quickly and every day that the property is yours you are paying interest. In my experience, it is often the case that they will ask for double the amount off that they will eventually accept.

This is where keeping good relationships when doing business becomes important, and the better you get on with them the less likely they will be to try their luck at this – normally if they feel as though they know you on a personal level, they will be too embarrassed. Also, a good agent pays at this point, as they can head off problems like this before they gain any real traction.

A few years ago, I was negotiating on behalf of my mother when she was moving home. I told my mother that the vendor was under real pressure to move, and I asked her if she wanted me to engage in the aforementioned tactic, and she said no in no uncertain terms. This wasn't because she didn't want a price reduction, but because she was only moving down the road and didn't want to bump into the vendor if they were to play bridge together!

However, most people will try this if their brave enough. If £5,000 in cash is put down on the table, human nature makes us want to pick it up.

Never be afraid to ask yourself questions. In this case, the most obvious question is, 'do you want the money in your bank as soon as possible?' With the next question being 'can you be flexible to make sure this happens?' The answer to both of these should always be yes. Unfortunately, sometimes other issues can get in the way, but refer back to this and make sure you feel as though you have a clear vision of your end goal.

CHAPTER 12
FUNDING DEALS

There are a number of ways of funding property deals, although if you are very lucky and have large cash funds available, the following doesn't really apply. However, if you are in the vast majority, there are options available to you, and if the deal is good enough you should be able to find a way to secure the finance and make this happen.

FINANCIAL BACKERS

Over the years I have been guilty of using my financial backers too often and not doing enough deals independently. However, the problem is, if you don't feed your financial backer, they will go out and find someone who can provide them with a regular stream of deals. It's a real advantage to have someone with financial clout behind you, this makes proving the funds needed to purchase a lot easier. This also means that they will deal with the financial aspects of the transaction, leaving you to focus on what you bring to the table – doing the deals.

I have worked with backers for over 35 years now, and I can say that I have never fallen out with any of them. And one way to ensure that you don't, is even when you aren't putting any of your own money into the deal you still take your share of the risk, any loss that arises from the deal should be agreed on the same basis as your share of the profit.

The agreement I have with most backers tends to be between 33% to 50% of net profit, but I take no money out of the transaction until the deal is totally complete and the proceeds are being shared out between everyone entitled.

If you begin wanting to take money out for expenses along the way you are in real danger of your backer losing confidence in you. You need to be seen as being financially secure and responsible, without the need for handouts as the project proceeds.

It is imperative that you are able to quickly gain the confidence and trust of your backer, and the best way to do this? Always under-promised and over-deliver. That way, when you go to them with a deal that is worth £300,000 and you deliver £310,00, they will have faith in you for the next deal.

Most backers will use a smaller deal first to decide whether you are worthy of this confidence of trust, and this is very sensible on their part. And, as you then get to know each other better they will feel more confidence lending you more money.

With any new backer, I recommend starting off with a small deal that you can pitch to them which will offer them a good return, but which you are still sure you can over-deliver on. This will serve you well for future deals.

Remember, if all goes well and you get along with them, it can result in both of you being able to make a lot of money together. Don't let greed spoil relationships on the first or the fifteenth deal.

Funding Deals

BANK FUNDING

For those of you who need complete control, the main banks are still an option, but realistically only if you're looking to borrow 50% or less of the purchase price. They also like to know your track record, and if you can't prove this to them you are far less likely to get the funding this way.

You also need to understand bank rates and fees. For example, when they tell you that they will lend you the money at 5% over base, there will also be costs for borrowing the money in the first place. These costs are normally 1-2% of the amount of the loan, and the same again when you complete on the sale and pay the money back to them. It all adds up, so make sure you know what you're doing, down to the last pound.

Furthermore, depending on who you're dealing with, it can take up to three-months for a bank to actually produce the money to you. One they have had your inside leg measurement and know your every monthly expense – probably down to how much you spend on a haircut – they will then as you to pay for a valuation, undertaken on their behalf!

If the valuation comes back favourably, they will then instruct their solicitors, and you guessed it…you'll also be paying for these on top of your own solicitor.

Remember, they have first charge on the property, which means they get their money back first. If you're buying three house, this means you might not see any money until the first two have completed, although you can try and negotiate so they take a percentage of each sale, and this is worth trying to discuss.

However, a word of caution, we did a similar deal on a block of twelve flats in Clacton-on-Sea during a recession, and when we sold the first one, they took all the money. We queried this and said we agreed to 80%, to which they informed us that we did at the time, but the terms have now changed. The banks have the prerogative to change their minds when an agreement like that is made, which may seem unfair but unfortunately, we don't have the bargaining power of a major lending institution.

Since the 2008 recession there have been numerous new banks start-up which specialise in property dealing. They charge you more to borrow the money but will get the funds to you far quicker and have been set up for exactly this purpose. We often use these as they will get the transaction completed in 28 days and commonly deal with the same type of issues that you or I can face. They will normally lend up to a maximum of 70 to 75% loan to value.

BRIDGING FINANCE

I warn you; this sort of lending is not for the faint-hearted or those who are risk averse. Bridging finance companies will normally lend up to 80% of purchase price and conclude the deal within 14 days. These institutions commonly deal with auction buyers who need quick decisions.

A common scenario where they will prove useful is in the case that you may have another property coming to market, but which has not yet sold, so you have not got the funds to purchase the property. They will charge you anywhere from 8% to 15% and will sometimes take on those without good credit history. However, as is always the case, the bigger the risk they are taking on your, the more they will charge you in interest. They don't normally lend for longer than 12 months, so you need to be sure you can repay in time, as they are more ruthless than other lenders and you will be placed under significantly more pressure.

PERSONAL GUARANTEES

For a lot of people, a personal guarantee is a particularly scary thought and, of course, in an ideal world you would never need to sign a personal guarantee to a bank. Prior to the 2008 recession I was very proud that I had no personal guarantees on any of my borrowing. However, that soon changed when the property market crashed. The banks then forced me into personal guarantees on our borrowing at the time, which of course I did my very best to argue against.

It is now near impossible to borrow money that doesn't require a personal guarantee in any form, even if it's not against the entire amount you are borrowing. My advice is to grin and bear it. If you have a spouse or partner, make sure they are aware of it, and that the bank doesn't insist on having a personal guarantee from them also.

Ultimately, a personal guarantee requires you to back yourself entirely and put your own money on the line as well as theirs, so from this perspective it makes sense even if it is somewhat nerve-wracking – especially when you are new to property dealings.

I have spoken a lot about the negative aspects of borrowing from a bank, but it is worth remembering that even if you are paying very high interest, it is still a lot cheaper than handing over between 50 and 80% of your profit to a financial backer.

BUILDING SOCIETIES

In the UK we are incredibly fortunate to have building societies, they were originally formulated as a non-profit organisation to lend on property. Most now work in much the same way as a bank, but they are still unique to the UK. Having these institutions is one of the reasons why the UK is such a great place to be investing in property making borrowing on money far easier than much of the rest of the world.

However, I would like to make it clear that I don't condone any investors using a traditional building society with lending to be repaid over 20 to 25 years if they intend to refurbish the property only to sell this on again. People who engage in this practice will put the property on the market, sell it and will do the same thing again. This isn't what a building society is intended for.

Of course, if you're living in the property yourself, refurbish, and then decide it isn't where you feel you want to call home, this is a different matter entirely. One sale won't trigger tax on the profit you've made on your own home.

And whilst I previously mentioned that I don't agree with this, neither will HMRC. Doing this on numerous occasions will likely be considered trading and as such will be subject to the normal UK taxes. Therefore, it is always advisable to retain receipts for all the costs you have incurred in the process of the refurbishment, just in case you are taxed on your profits you can offset these costs at least.

BUY-TO-LET MORTGAGES

One of the reasons why the buy-to-let market has really exploded since the turn of the century is because of this way of borrowing. Prior to that, it was really for those who like me are professional property investors; those who would use traditional banks to buy properties to rent out.

The introduction of buy-to-let markets has opened this sector of the market to so many more people, and at a higher loan to value ratio than we were previously able to get.

Buy-to-let lenders seem to be fairly happy if there is a 50% margin between the rental value and mortgage repayments. But it is worth remembering that the 50% is not just pure profit, this is also to allow for all the other associated costs, including general repairs, insurance, tax and rent voids – periods where the property is either vacant or the tenant isn't paying.

However, despite all of the above factors, some people have managed to build up extensive residential portfolios, and in a period when property values are increasing a large portfolio can be built fairly quickly. One way of doing this is to refinance every few years and use any cash raised to buy more property. Although I must warn you, it's all very well until the music stops.

When you see that property price increases are beginning to slow my advice is to reduce the loans you have. Reduce your loans to a more sensible value, bringing them down to 50% of the value of each property, meaning that the loans are very easily covered by any rent coming in on them.

In this case, quickly decide which properties you wish to dispose of and get them on the market straight away and, I cannot emphasise this enough, do not wait for the highest possible price – especially in a market that is dropping. Other people may not realise the market is dropping as quickly as you being to take notice, but they soon will. And take it from someone who has a property career that has spanned multiple recessions, act quickly because as soon as everyone knows it's happening you need to be in a secure position.

PRIVATE LOANS

When interest rates are desperately low there are more people willing to lend you money privately. They're normally those that already know you and are receiving less than 1% interest at the bank or building society. They will be delighted to receive 6 to 10% interest per annum from you if the risk is minimal and short term.

Like with a financial backer, you are better to borrow small amounts at first and build up their confidence in you – rather than borrowing too much too quickly and scaring them away on a risky investment. They may not be commercially minded individuals, so you need to gain their trust. And, again, this leaves more of the profit to you than having a backer.

MORTGAGE BROKER

A good mortgage broker is worth their weight in gold. I have spoken previously about having a 'team', and a broker is an essential part of this – along with your estate agent and solicitor. Great mortgage brokers can be characterised as hard-working, helpful, responsive and importantly, know their market inside out.

There are a number of specialist pop-up lenders that have come to the fore since the last recession, and most are only accessible via your mortgage broker. These lenders don't have a high street presence, so there's a good chance you aren't even aware of them and so a knowledgeable financial broker's importance cannot be underestimated.

Some good mortgage brokers will charge you a fee for finding you the right mortgage, and all will receive a fee from the building society or bank. However, don't begrudge a fee to anyone who helps you – it's very short sighted.

A mortgage broker may also suggest a number of add-ons where they can earn further commission, for example redundancy insurance. Just be aware of this, some products may be useful to you, others may not, and if you do take advantage of these products make sure you fully understand what they are and when they are useful to you. It's like when you buy a TV or a washing machine, sometimes you might want the extended warranty and sometimes you take your chances, it depends on costs and your own temperament.

If you build up a good rapport with your mortgage broker, they almost become your funding partner, but again at a far more affordable rate than a financial backer.

FAMILY

Finally, there is always family. And when writing this I do understand that this is not an option for everyone, but if it is please do read on.

This may well be your first port-of-call when trying to raise money to buy an investment property and, in many cases, could be your best prospect. You should always bear in mind, though, if you have siblings or other family members, they may not be so pleased that your family members are lending you the money, and not them.

Although there may still be some initial discomfort, the way to overcome this is to treat your family as though they are any other investor. To do this, you should offer them the same interest or the same profit share as you would if you were borrowing the money from anyone else. This way, their lending you money appears fairer to other family members and means that if you need them to do the same again and they remain in the position to do so, I am sure they will.

On a more personal note, we all have to start somewhere. On my 18th birthday, my mother lent me a small amount of money which I used to buy my first two investment properties. I paid her interest and then gave her a share of the profit, which she was delighted to receive. And guess what? She lent me some more money the next time to do another death. And for this, I will always be incredibly grateful. She believed in me from a young age, and this has enabled my achievements since.

INHERITANCE

If you are fortunate to have some inheritance coming to you in the future, particularly if this is money in a trust, it could be worth discussing whether having this sooner is possible. Explaining why this money could be helpful to you know and how it would allow you to get on the investment ladder is important.

And, as most people are aware, depending on the size of the inheritance there can also be a saving of 40% inheritance tax should the person gifting it to you live for another seven years or more. However, please take professional advice on this as legislation is subject to change.

I appreciate that this is a difficult conversation, but if you want to deal and invest in property, then the ability to be forthright and ask the tough questions could be essential when trying to make a deal happen. This difficult conversation could be the boost needed to make yourself a lot of money in the future, and the person bequeathing the inheritance may be very pleased to see you putting the money to good us. So, ask!

CHAPTER 13
LOCATION

I am often asked where to buy for the best rental returns in the UK. There isn't one answer to this, and if I were to give an answer this is subject to change. However, I can give you some of the factors that you should consider when you are deciding where to make your investment.

The clear answer is to buy close to where you live, there are a number of advantages. Not least of which is you know the local market, you know the people, and being able to keep your ear close to the ground gives you an advantage over people coming in from another area.

Although, it is easy to forget the bigger picture. You need to remain unbiased about your local area, but you do have the advantage of knowing this past and future of the place where you live, for example if there are plans for a new road, this can be used to your advantage.

Over the last 40 years, I probably haven't bought enough property in my local area. Instead, I have always been willing to travel throughout the UK to get the best profit margins I can find. Sometimes I have perhaps pushed a little too hard, when I may have done just as well by staying strong on my own patch. This is something that over the last few years I have made the effort to try to change.

Unless you have the advantage of being incredibly wealthy, or have found an amazing financial backer, there is generally little point in trying to find big deals in London where prices are extraordinarily high. One of my regrets, I should have bought in London when I first began investing.

You really need to decide whether you're going for a high return on your outlay, in which case, buying in some of the cheaper areas of the country, such as parts of the north will give you a brilliant return on your money. You can probably look to achieve a 10% yield in certain areas.

The downside to this, is that you won't get the same capital growth. As a general rule, the better the rental return, the worse the capital growth, although there are of course exceptions. In other words, if you bought something for £50k five years ago, it might only be worth £55k today, but in the meantime, you've had a good rental return.

If you pick better parts of the country (including some parts of the north again) you will find that your rental return isn't as good, but if you keep paying the mortgage for five years, you'll discover a much better return on your capital. You will also be paying more for the property to begin with, and so outlaying more capital.

A great deal of property which is let to people who are out of work, and so paid for by the state, differs little in terms of rental income from county to county, apart from in London. This may change in the future, but certainly makes the areas where you

Location

can get a little more for your money more attractive for this type of property.

Don't buy properties that you see boarded up, as it means that there's little need for rental properties there. You may think everyone else has missed a trick, but this is unlikely. You will probably find that the windows are smashed and you're needing to board them up before you've even found a tenant. You will find yourself in a vicious circle.

If you live in a majority of the home counties, it is difficult to understand that in other parts of the country there is little demand for rental properties in other parts of the county. Please do not buy in these areas. There is an old saying: "when buying horses, spend as much as you can afford as good horses make good riders." And the same can be said of property and tenants, why buy something that's going to cause you trouble?

Please don't get offended when I generalise about different areas. But, if a terraced house in Burnley is £20k, I can assure there is a very good reason, and if you are hearing about it then there's probably a reason why somebody else hasn't yet snapped it up.

If you do go to a town, you an unfamiliar with, jump in a taxi and ask them to drive you around the local area for ten minutes and in this time, you'll find out more than you will ever get out of any agent – and you'll certainly find out about the no-go areas of the town.

So far, I've run you through all the challenges of buying rental property outside of your area, but this is not to say that it can also be a successful venture. I don't want to put anyone off, because I have been successful in doing so, but pick a very good area of the town to buy in, and to do this you need to know the town.

People often say to me, "I don't want to buy a property 200 miles away from where I live, because I'll never be able to see it." My answer to this is simple – this is a business. If it's well managed by the local property management company, why on earth do you need to look at it? You're not planning on living in it, so it shouldn't matter to you where it is.

25 years ago, I bought five flats on the Isle of Wight. My brother joked at the time, "I thought the Isle of Wight was a tax haven?" In those 25 years, I have visited them twice, and they've gone up five-fold in value – I rest my case.

UNIVERSITY CITIES

Over the last few decades there has been a huge growth in the proportion of the population going to university, and because of this the number of university places available, and in turn – the number of students needing to rent accommodation. This has given the property investor a great opportunity to get better yields on what would otherwise be pretty average property stock.

Student accommodation is often subsidised by student loans or the bank of mum and dad, and the pressure on housing stock close to universities has made it a very attractive investment, often accommodating six or so people into one house.

A word of warning – if you are thinking of going down this route, you should ensure that you have the latest regulations from your local authority. You must be aware that should there be a fire or some other problem in the property, not having these adequate protections puts you at real risk of being sued by your tenants. Your insurance cover will not be worth much if you are not compliant with all the regulations.

The good news is that the high-level of rents paid by students in university cities means that even in a recession your investment will be adequately underwritten. Even if there should be a downturn in property prices or rent yield, such accommodation is always in high demand.

To ensure that rent is always paid we always ask for a guarantee from the parents of the students. This is not just for rent, but also to cover the condition of the property when it is returned to us. There can be no 'fingers crossed and hope for the best' attitude when it comes to renting a property, especially to students.

This opens up another opportunity for investment, if your son or daughter is at university, buying a house and renting it out to their friends while they are at university can be a very clever move. But, like any investment, take into account the market and that property prices aren't going down, also that they have good friends that will pay their rent and take care of the property.

CHAPTER 14
CHOOSING TENANTS

Choosing tenants is a very difficult job. If you're not local to the property or have a very large portfolio you are unlikely to meet them. If you are local, I suggest meeting them as this could save you a lot of trouble and frustration. Just because the property management company tells you they are acceptable and the references are good, this doesn't mean they will look after the property well.

I have some wonderful friends, but not all of them are as clean and tidy as I would hope or expect and most of them have money. Even some of the people I know and like I can still say I probably wouldn't choose as tenants.

Don't just rely on references. If you can, get your property management company to carry out inspections every three to six months, and if the property isn't being kept in good order for a pre-planned inspection – get rid of the tenants. They aren't only going to bring down the value of the property, but you'll spend time and money doing remedial works to put things right again before it can be re-let.

It's all very well for the property management company to say that they have a deposit, but a deposit doesn't go very far when you have to redecorate and repair.

My advice, if you have let them in but realise you've made a mistake, is to get them out as soon as possible. It is better to lose a month or so of no rent than to have months of lost rent while you undertake repairs.

When it comes to choosing a property management company to look after your properties, do your research and ask a lot of questions of the company before you let them look after your property. This isn't a decision you want to get wrong.

As I previously mentioned, regular inspections are important. Whilst these inspections may cost you money, normally they offer great value for money, and I normally agree with their fees that are offered and don't try to haggle them down. And, like when working with an estate agent to sell my property, I believe that compensating people well will make them want to work for you. Firstly, I want them to rent my property out as a priority and secondly, I want them to look after it.

Many years ago, when I was in my mid 20s, I started selling properties to the Granger trust – which at the time was one of the biggest landlords in the UK – owning something like 25,000 properties. And at the time I couldn't understand why their rents were so competitive. I thought that if I ever owned that many properties I would want to get as much rent for each property as possible, however I now realise that I would have been totally wrong.

The reason they charged such competitive rates was that it was very important to them that they kept their occupancy rates as high as possible. They didn't want lots of empty properties around the country, this leaves them open to vandalism and damp. By keeping rents competitive, they were able to get another tenant in quickly if one tenant moved out, something they wouldn't have been able to do if they tried to get maximum rental income from each individual property.

The moral of the story is, if you have good tenants, do your utmost to keep them in the property. If they move out because you've increased the rent, any increase you might have been made will be lost by having the property empty. Also remember that as soon as the property is vacant it's likely to not look so attractive – in need of redecorating, carpets cleaning, and so on.

This reminds me of another old saying, 'happy wife, happy life.' Happy tenants reduce your stress and give you the best rental return.

CHAPTER 15
REFURBISHMENTS

Now for the fun part – buying to convert or refurbishing existing residential properties. This has really been the mainstay of my business for the last 40 years.

Putting builders and trades aside for the moment, it's very easy to think that a building won't cost much to either convert or refurbish. You are likely to be excited, optimistic and highly motivate to take on the project. I don't want to put you off the prospect, but in those 40 years I don't think I have had a project come in on time or under budget. I've managed one or the other, but never at the same time.

A very simple rule of thumb that applies to new buildings as well as refurbishment, is that you can never really afford to pay more than 30 to 35% of the end value on furnishings and decorations.

This may sound tough to achieve, but I assure that such properties are out there.

You really need a full schedule of works to be done, so that the builder knows exactly what he is quoting on. That way there is no argument, and each builder is pricing on the same job each time.

Of course, if there is just a bit of decorating and a new bathroom to fit this is quite a different scenario to a full refurbishment. By a full refurbishment I mean everything from the roof, windows, wiring all the way to the bathroom, kitchen and replastering.

To do this, you need a building surveyor. For this job, you shouldn't use an architect, and whilst they may well tell you they can cope with the whole job, you need someone who is a little more hard-nosed and has the skills to deal with another tradesman. Architects are normally very talented and nice people who will do an excellent job of designing, you need someone who can deal with the practicalities.

A good, strong-minded building surveyor might charge up to 10% of the value of the job. And if they do, they are well worth the money. You don't need to be dealing with builders on a day-to-day basis with the builders. Part of the job will be to value the works that have been carried out and confirm payment when satisfied. I don't know of any builder that has every undervalued an interim invoice, so to save yourself a headache – get yourself a good building surveyor.

When you first have a look around, if you see any movement above the doorway or any cracks whatsoever, I recommend that you get a structural engineer to have a quick look – even if this is after the exchange of contracts. Remember, there are two types of structural engineers; the first is the type too scared to cross the road because he might get run over, and the second is more pragmatic and will give you sensible advice to overcome the problem.

Over the years, I have learned the cost of the two different types, and on occasion I have had a second opinion, which normally is very different from the first one. However, if you find the latter kind of structural engineer, please take his advice.

And, whilst I am on the subject, if you literally do 'paper over the cracks' as it were, someone will notice and have a fully survey done so don't try and wing it. It used to be that you could sometimes hide a crack with a little render, this is no longer normally the case.

SALES TIPS FOR RENOVATIONS

I could write a book on its own and regurgitate the same information as number of popular TV shows telling you to put the coffee on, bake some bread and hang some nice curtains – but I hope you have realised by now I hope to give you some more practical advice that is based on years of trial and error.

There are plenty of 'experts' who will advise you on colour schemes and the like, but unless you're doing a show home on a larger development, you need to be focusing on the money first and foremost. Additionally, when the house is vacant a lot of these things won't apply anyway.

There are some things that can make a big difference when renovating a property, small things that can take your project from average to being professionally finished. Firstly, whilst it might be very tempting, never use second-hand materials of any sort or go for the cheapest choice. Particularly for kitchens and bathrooms choosing something that is a decent quality will make a big difference.

Another thing that may seem obvious to ensuring that everything is to the best possible standard is to check that the painters have also done the inside of the cupboards. Similarly, check the windows haven't been painted over.

The standard of living has increased vastly in the last 20 years, and I'm sure that to many some of my housing stock looks rather dated. Now, most people seem to want a property to look like a show home or a hotel when they move in.

If the house is terraced, you should make sure there are fire walls between this property and the neighbouring one, and that it is very well insulated. It was said that many affairs would take place between householders when people could climb into the loft, walk along a few houses and then drop down into their lover's landing – although I can't personally attest to this!

I digress. As you can see, successful selling begins with the finish. It needs to look sharp, clean and kept in simple colours. Another recommendation, when you are changing the doors, don't go for the cheapest – for a little more you can get solid oak doors. You want them to 'clunk' as you close them.

Carpets are another area where people often go wrong. The best thing you can do is to put down underlay, this is very cheap and will allow you to put down a cheaper carpet. When buyers come round to view your development it will feel like Axminster, but at a fraction of the price.

Make sure that all lights have shades – you'll be amazed at the difference this can make.

If the property has a cellar, do not get sucked into spending money on this. Clean and white was it. If there is damp this really doesn't matter as it's below ground level. Market this area as storage only as you don't want viewers to be immediately disappointed. Some people get tempted into tanking cellars and basements which is very expensive and is unlikely to make the room any more habitable. Basically, it's a complete waste of money.

If the property has a basement with windows, you could consider making it into a habitable room. However, in my experience, the above point still stands it's normally a waste of money. And, moreover, it sometimes makes potential buyers believe you've missed a trick. Although, if you do try, be aware that it's very difficult to keep the basement dry, and the guarantees from companies that tank basements with waterproof render needs to be carefully read.

Something that you always need to be mindful of is making it as easy as possible to get that house sold. If there is a garden it should be clean and tidy and if fences are rotten, they need to be replaced. Builders are notorious for not getting rid of the last bits of rubbish, so make sure this is cleared up immediately. The garden doesn't need to be thoughtfully landscaped, but a bit of turf and some painted fences will make a complete difference. And whilst I'm on the topic of fences, gates shouldn't be rusty, and pathways can easily have a new layer of pea shingle or gravel. All of these are cheap solutions, that can cover a multitude of sins and, most importantly, make the difference when it comes to selling your property.

Another point, even if the actual fence isn't yours but looks a mess, ask the neighbour if they mind you replacing it. Don't be stubborn and refuse just because it isn't yours – pride comes before a fall. Many times, I have replaced the boundary to neighbouring properties, or offered to paint the front of their house whilst doing mine.

If you are undertaking any electrical works, and rewiring in particular, you should ensure that the electrician is fully qualified and that you will receive a certificate at the end of the job. This will need to be given to your solicitor and inserted into the sales pack. Additionally, the boiler needs to be registered with the relevant local authority and in the sales pack, along with any guarantees for other household appliances. It is amazing how many times we have managed to lose the guarantees for fridges or cookers etc, so be methodical and organised.

Finally, once the carpets are down, we get what is called a builder's clean, by which I definitely do not mean your builder does it – as we all know this would likely be a complete mess. You should arrange this with a professional cleaning company, they need to clean everywhere including the windows – inside and out. And, if for any reason it doesn't sell quickly, make sure you keep it clean and tidy, and that any post or junk mail is regularly seen to.

CHAPTER 16
LISTED BUILDINGS

I have renovated many listed buildings over the years, but this isn't something I would always recommend, and especially not if you are just getting started. Any issues you can encounter with the normal renovation of a house are magnified by it being either Grade II or Grade II* listed. I have only ever renovated one Grade I house, and all I have to say is…never again!

Anything and everything you want to do will be scrutinised, which is correct as it's an important historical building, but this will only make your life harder.

I recently purchased an old YMCA in Norwich, which is a Grade II* listed building. I subsequently obtained planning permission and sold it to someone who had never undertaken a conversion before, certainly a brave individual. They had the good sense to ask me to act as a consultant on the project. He wanted to alter the existing planning, changing it to six, two-bedroomed apartments and one townhouse. I was able to bring my team of experts in to make sure the project went smoothly, which it did, however I cannot be everywhere, so my advice is please do not attempt to do it.

Obtaining listed building consent is long and arduous and requires a very good architect with specialist knowledge in listed buildings. Even then there can be numerous meetings and negotiations that take place with the conservation department of the council as they are looking for a perfect solution, however with an old building you constantly have to compromise. And this makes finding where you can agree exceptionally tough.

Never start to develop a listed building without the listed building consent in place. If you do, you will very quickly have an enforcement notice served on you and will have to stop work. I will also choose this moment to remind you that this is a criminal offence, and you would be liable.

CHAPTER 17
CONSERVATION AREAS

And the topic of listed buildings brings me onto another tricky department, conservation areas – these can be nearly as problematic for a developer.

Many years ago, I owned a piece of land next to a block of flats. At one time in the past the land had a building on it, so I wanted to apply for planning permission. There were some cherry trees on the site, I asked my chap to remove the cherry trees and clear the site which he did. I then had a notice served on me very quickly by the council stating that I had removed trees without permission. These trees did not have a tree preservation order on them so I assumed I could just take them down, however because they were in a conservation area, I needed permission.

I ended up going along to what I thought was a council tribunal. However, when I got there, they had appointed a barrister and it was a court hearing! I had no legal representation, so I explained to the judge it was a genuine mistake which she accepted and only fined me £2000 as I'd already replaced the trees and apologised for my mistake. The maximum they could have fined me then was £20,000. I'm sure it's even higher now, so beware and ask if it is a conservation area or not before you buy!

The rule of thumb is if it's in a nice area, it probably is a conservation area so planning will be more difficult, but nothing like the challenge of listed buildings. You can find out more detail about where conservation areas are by looking at the relevant local authority's website.

CHAPTER 18
BUILDINGS WITH ENFORCEMENT NOTICES

An enforcement notice is served when there has been a breach of planning control, this notice can require you to make changes to the property, stop work and sometimes demolish work that has been undertaken. In some cases, these aren't as bad as they sound. If you look to buy property with them on just make sure that you can get the work done to get the notices lifted easily without a fight from the council.

You need to understand the work required by the enforcement officer and that you are prepared to carry out the work as stipulated. The good news is that this may well put off a large number of purchasers, but personally I wouldn't be too daunted by this so long as you intend to do the work in a professional manner.

Ensure you get the enforcement officer back to check the work and make sure he signs it off as completed and that it is registered as such. There is nothing worse than getting a buyer and their solicitor to tell you that there is still a notice on the building for works to be carried out, knowing that you have already done all those works but that the notice has not been lifted. It quite often happens if the enforcement officer moves on to another job. It is your responsibility to make sure that the notice has been lifted from the property in a proper legal way, so double check that it has been done prior to any sale.

Enforcement notices are often put on a property where the owner is absent or has financial difficulty and can't carry out repairs required to bring the building up to standard. Or it could be that a structure which has not got planning permission has been built within the curtilage of the building.

CHAPTER 19
DEALING WITH BUILDERS AND OTHER TRADESMEN

We have all heard some horrific stories about builders and other tradesmen. In my experience, most builders are decent and want to do a good job. The biggest problem is that they don't like saying no or to turn work down because they are always worried about keeping their men busy as they have to pay them whether they are busy or not.

The strategy of most small builders is to have three jobs on at any one time, with each client unaware that there are two other jobs happening. As I said, you can't really blame them, as they don't know when the tap is going to be switched off as it were.

When you get to your property, perhaps on a Wednesday to check on the work and there is just one person there it can be very frustrating as time is money. The longer it takes to get the job done, the less you might make because of the interest payments, so you need to continually drive the job forward.

Giving a builder a timescale to do the job within is a good start. The timescale needs to be agreed with the builder, rather than you dictating to him. You need to try and create a working partnership to mutual benefit. The sooner he finishes the job the sooner his team can move onto another one, although as I mentioned before they may well have already started on the next before yours is complete.

As I said before, if it's a bigger job then it's essential to have a building surveyor hold your hand through the process. For a smaller job, you really are on your own because it's not worth employing a surveyor and they probably wouldn't be interested in taking the work on anyway.

Don't always go for the cheapest quote. Have a look at the other work the builder has done and try to talk to the owner or other interested party to see if they've done it within the correct timescale.

Always make sure you write down everything you want done and that each builder is pricing up the same amount of work on a like-for-like basis, otherwise clearly you will have a distorted view of the prices. Having in writing what you have agreed leaves no room for debate.

Never settle on an open-ended agreement or on day work or suchlike. Even if you think you know and trust them it is open to all sorts of problems and disagreements. The key to all this is to finish the job quickly and as efficiently and economically as you can. You will not achieve that if you have any disagreements whatsoever with the builder. I implore you to always try to maintain positive working relationships where possible.

You wouldn't cross the road with your eyes shut. So never enter into any agreement with a builder not knowing what the final costs will be.

Assuming you have listened to the above and have a fixed price off them that you're happy with, make sure that you don't overpay them on a monthly basis. The trick that some of them get up to is to overcharge for the work they have done early on, which helps with their cash flow, but leaves very little incentive for them to finish the job at the end.

Make sure by the time the job is finished you still have at least 15 to 20% in hand which you can give them upon total completion of the job. When I say completely finished, I mean *completely* finished, including everything being clean and tidy. The most important thing at the end is the snagging list. You need to go around on your own, without the builder, writing down in each room what needs to be finished correctly. There will be lots of small, little things that aren't right, and this is quite normal. Do not start this process until they have confirmed they have finished.

When you give him your snagging list, hand it to the builder asking him to work through the list. When he says he's done it, go back and check. If things still aren't quite right, write out another snagging list to get it finally finished. Only at the point when it is all completed to the agreement and your satisfaction, do you pay him the final payment. Make sure that the builder has registered the boiler with the council, as previously mentioned, and that you have received all of the relevant guarantees from him.

Whatever the agreed fee for the building contract allow an extra 10% for any genuine extras there may be on a renovation. It's very difficult to be completely accurate on a fixed price. For instance, when they pull off the rotten skirting boards or uncover the original fireplace, they don't know what they're going to find underneath.

Some discoveries of course may put the value of the property up and make it more saleable, but just always allow 10% extra to ensure you can comfortably cover the full cost of the works.

Always try to wait until the end of the contract to agree any extra costs, unless it's a large item. At this point, the work will already have been done and you are in a much stronger position to negotiate when the job is finished, and the house is on the market than halfway through when you need it finished.

Don't pick a builder that you have met socially and stuck up a rapport with. You're not looking for a friend, you're looking for someone to enter into business transactions with. Be friendly and helpful, but if you have a partner or spouse do not let them interfere and put you or the builder under too much pressure, otherwise you are in danger of him walking off the job.

He will inevitably be late in finishing the job so if you agree with him to do it in three months allow four and a half months. That way although it will be frustrating you will quietly have a smile on your face that is being done on time, or at least when you really expected it to be done!

Don't give him any excuses for being late, such as you are changing the specification halfway through. You are better to take a little longer before starting to get the specifications absolutely right, rather than changing your mind at any point. Not only will it give him the excuse that he can't get it done on time, but he will also charge you dearly for the changes as he's already the one on site so you can't get anyone else in to do them.

Dealing with Builders and Other Tradesmen

Some people might try to save money by employing a builder for the building work only, opting to coordinate all the other trades, such as plumbers and electricians themselves. In my experience, you are best to leave the builder to organise the whole job and to coordinate all the trades. He may charge you extra on top of what the plumber would charge you directly, or he may not, but either way if it's not done on time, it's his responsibility and you have only person to deal with, not five.

Always remember, interest is accruing on the money you have borrowed so even if one builder is slightly more expensive than another, if he's going to perform quickly for you, he's worth employing. Quicker means less hassle, less stress and more profit.

One trick I've used over the years is to tell the builder that the carpets are being put down a week or so earlier than they actually are. You never have to admit that you've done it, because they will never be ready the week earlier, but it gives them a push so that hopefully they are ready the week after when the carpets actually booked in. And then, you can tell them that you've done them a favour and put it back a week.

At least we are not in France…a friend of mine recently went over to do a large fencing contract for a lady who'd moved over to France with her horses. My friend did the fencing work in nine days; the local French fencing contractor wanted six weeks. The French builder decided he would leave off work a day early for his four-week annual closedown in August leaving her with no running water which he could have got done if he had left when he said he was going too.

He just said in broken English that he would do it on his return to work on 1st September! Having heard this story, I've become a lot more grateful for the English builder.

CHAPTER 20
CHOOSING A SOLICITOR AND ESTATE AGENT

Some people will say that it doesn't really matter who your solicitor is as it's a straightforward legal transaction. But let me tell you, as someone who has purchased over 4,000 properties throughout my career, a poor solicitor/conveyancer will lose you money by not acting quickly enough or not saving a transaction that could otherwise be. Their bad advice and inactivity will waste your money and time and cost you deals.

It really doesn't matter whether you choose a fully qualified solicitor or a licensed conveyancer who concentrates purely on property transactions. Just make sure that whoever you choose is good!

There is a real fashion to choose a cheap conveyancer, from what I call conveyancing factories. These have been set up to deal with high volumes of transactions. You don't know who is dealing with yours personally and they work within a computer framework, so there is no personal interaction. You can't even speak to them on the phone. I strongly advise you do not use one of these firms.

You need to choose a solicitor or licensed conveyancer who you can meet in person, who will keep you fully advised all the way through the transaction by email or telephone and who has the authority to make decisions on the spot, rather than have to go through a manager.

Mark Hayward who has been my solicitor for 25 years or more emails me on a Sunday and has exchanged contracts for me while he's lying on a beach in Barbados on his Blackberry. He is generally available to me 16-hours a day. I'm not expecting you to find someone who is prepared to do that for you, but you certainly need to make sure that the person you choose is interested in what he or she does and is committed to giving you the best possible service.

Do not go for the cheapest and make sure you like them, and they get on with you. Do not choose one that has only just qualified. They won't have the experience required, so let them make their mistakes with someone else, not you!

It really needs to be a partnership. Only bother him when you need to contact him, as much as possible by email rather than telephone. Then, if you do telephone when you need to get hold of him, he will realise it is important.

Once you get your property 'under offer', it is then that the real work starts. **At the estate agent offices I own, we have a sales progression department** whose sole role is to work with the solicitor on your behalf to get the deal through as quickly and as smoothly as possible.

Some agents do realise the true benefit of these sales progressors. When you're choosing an agent to handle your property, try to find one that has such people in the team and ask for a weekly update

Choosing a Solicitor and Estate Agent

from them. Like a good solicitor, these people can save deals. You can then liaise with the solicitor should there be anything that is not being done quickly enough.

One of my pet hates is that the local search is not carried out on the property until the mortgage offer has been received from the buyer. This drives me mad because it slows down the sale.

What I do to counter this is to pay for a search on my own property. They last three to six months and I then pass it across to the buyer along with all the enquiry and property forms filled in. I get these done prior to the sale even being agreed. That way, when you know who the solicitor is that's acting for the other side, you can send him a full pack of legal documents.

You can agree to a 21-day exchange of contracts when agreeing the sale. As with the builder, we all know it probably won't happen in 21-days, but at least if you set this target, it is far more likely to be done within the month. Make it as easy as possible for the sale to go through by not putting any obstacles in the way. As I mentioned before, always do everything you can possibly do. Every day that you own the property is another day of interest you're paying.

As I've mentioned before, if you've purchased the property that you are now selling through an agent, it's the done thing to give it back to the same agent to resell it for you. This helps to ensure you continue to get deals from them; it's really the unspoken word in property dealing.

However, that doesn't mean you have to be weak with them. In terms of sale commission anything between one and one and a half per cent is standard and, in my experience, you don't get any better service by paying two percent. Be careful not to sign a sole agency agreement for more than 4 to 6 weeks as keeps the agent on their toes and motivates them to get a sale agreed within that time period. As I've said, many times before, time is money. Also, be sure not to pay any upfront fees for advertising or other ancillary items that they may suggest, as it is not necessary. You need to think, if they have already been paid, what are they working towards if not a commission?

You want them to price your property to find a buyer within 28-days. That will concentrate their mind and not put it on the market overpriced, which of course is the oldest trick in the world with agents, to stop you going to anyone else they are known to employ a little flattery.

Don't be concerned if they no longer use paper advertising as this went out with the Ark. It's all about being online with property search portals but do let them put up a 'For Sale' board - its old fashioned but it works!

Of course, an agent can never win. If he sells it to someone within the first few days, he has under-priced it, but if he has nobody is interested after one month, he has overpriced it. Whilst a property that isn't selling is almost always overpriced, sometimes a quick sale actually means it's priced correctly.

One modern way of marketing your property is to suggest an open house where the property is marketed for two weeks prior to the date of the open house. The intention is that you get as many people around it as you can to create some competition. Not all agents like to undertake this form of marketing, but it can be very successful within a town or city. The trick is to not let anybody view the property before the open day. They will try and say all sorts, such as they can't make the day because it's their daughter's birthday, but if they're keen, they will turn up.

If you have two buyers, clearly you want to pick the one who can proceed quickly. Your agent should do their due diligence on both buyers and have them prove cash funds or that they have a mortgage already arranged. If there is a chain of sales down the line you also want to know that they all have a sale on their houses that are able to proceed. Your agent should double check this by speaking to as many agents within the chain as they are able to.

A good agent will do this automatically for you and follow the sale through on a weekly basis giving you an update as selling the house is just as much a part of their job as finding you the buyer.

Over the years I had so many people ask me why their house hasn't sold. I ask them all the same question: how long has it been on the market? They might say nine-months, six-months or a year, but my answer to them is always the same. Every property in the UK sells if its priced right, whatever it is. You may be able to make it a lot easier to sell but they all sell at the right money. I've heard every excuse under the sun as to why their house has not sold, but the hard fact is that if it is priced correctly - it would have sold a long time ago.

If after a month we haven't sold a property that we have on the market, unless there is a high level of interest in it, I reduce it.

There is no point kidding yourself. It doesn't actually matter in the end what you think it's worth or what the agent thinks it's worth, the only person whose opinion matters is the person who is going to make an offer on it. Of course, you don't have to accept the offer, that is a judgement that you have to make with the advice of your agent.

When you do receive an offer, remember their first price is very rarely their last. If it is their only offer and you refuse it, you can take some comfort from the fact that they were probably never going to buy it in the first place. Just like if they view it for the third time, it's unlikely they will proceed. They will be trying to find reasons as to why they shouldn't buy.

It's a little like when there's a general election looming. It's the only excuse someone might need who is less keen to move than their partner, saying they are 'not sure what the country is going to be like after the election'. The fact is, it's very rare that a general election will affect a great deal of people and certainly not within the first months or so after it.

When you receive an offer, never sound relieved or excited. Remember, it doesn't matter to the agent what price he gets for

Choosing a Solicitor and Estate Agent

your property; the difference in his commission is negligible but it makes a lot of difference to you.

The first question I ask is how much the buyer will go up to. The answer you get is sometimes 'a whole lot more', in which case why are they asking you in the first place! However, you need to play the game. Suggest they come back to you with their best price. Once you have that you can then use that as the base price to negotiate from, you have instantly increased the offer without committing to a particular figure.

I use the tactic of splitting the difference from my asking price to where they are. Once I think I'm getting close to their maximum figure it squeezes a little bit more out of the deal for me. Should there then be any issue between the sale being agreed and exchange of contracts whereby I need to reduce the price slightly, it's hopefully only going to be by the extra that I managed to squeeze out of them and I'm happy to accept that if need be.

Remember, don't be like a builder who as I've said before thinks his house is the best house in the world because he's built it. Be sensible as pride always comes before a fall. Always be thinking about the next deal. Hopefully you've already got it in mind what you are going to buy next, so be practical and don't be greedy. If you're making a good profit, accept a compromise and get on with it and remember put them on the timescale I've suggested.

If there is a problem during the period between agreeing the sale and exchange, such as the building society valuer down valuing the property slightly, or them discovering another problem, try and rectify this quickly with a smile on your face. If you can't, suggest you meet on the cost of doing so. If it's a down valuation, use the agent as much as you can to lose as little as you can off the original price.

And as I mentioned before, finding a buyer is only the beginning of the process and there is some work to do before you reach the finish line – which is rarely easy. Be pleasant, persuasive and flexible. Hopefully by now you have chosen a really good solicitor and a really good agent who can make all the difference in helping the sale go as smoothly as possible.

A WORD OF WARNING

Please do not contemplate using an online agent. First of all, you have to pay an upfront fee whether they sell it for you or not, so you could be wasting your time and money. Secondly, they are unlikely to give you a genuine price on what your house is worth because they just want to get you to pay the fee upfront. Whether they sell it or not is irrelevant. As I mentioned before, this upfront fee will limit their motivation to get your property sold.

Additionally, as we know getting a buyer is just the start of the process. A good traditional agent, with a sales progression team behind him, will work night and day for you to get your property completed because If he doesn't, he gets paid nothing. The same cannot be said for online agents.

CHAPTER 21
BUYING AND SELLING AT AUCTION

Buying and selling at auction has become a far more popular form of buying and selling in the last 10 years and it's why, along with my business partner, I purchased Auction House UK during the 2009 recession. We grew the business from seven franchises to over 40 and became the leading UK auctioneers – in terms of the number of properties sold annually.

20 to 30 years ago I used to go to auctions and know quite a few people there. In fact, if you arrived late and missed the lot you wanted to buy you could quite often buy it off the person who just bought it, if they were happy to take a small profit, as we were all property dealers.

I mentioned in an earlier chapter that there are a few tricks that people used to use in the old days when going to auctions to buy, like asking a question in the room before the lot you're interested comes up, such as asking whether there is a report on the structure of the building, therefore suggesting that there could be a structural problem with it, even when you know there is not.

At our auctions, we don't allow anyone to ask any questions, so we have stopped that game. Being a property dealer means that you are aware of the tricks that others may employ to their advantage. Another that I mentioned earlier was removing the legal pack which sits on the tables of the lot you're interested in and not giving it back so no one else can look at it. It's not so effective now as most people have already looked online.

These things just don't happen anymore. Most of the rooms are filled with people like yourselves who are looking to invest in a house or to renovate and resell it and I'm absolutely delighted you are there. The numerous property shows have opened the market to many more people giving them the confidence to be able to buy at auctions.

The great thing when buying at auction is that the legal packs - the part that some solicitors take three-months or more to sort out - are all online, including the search so your solicitor can quickly and easily do the relevant due diligence.

With the confidence that you have taken legal advice, viewed the property, got a price for any work that is needed and have the funding in place, you are well set to purchase at auction.

Remember the guide price is purely that - a guide price. If it is between two figures, for example between £100,000 and £120,000 then the reserve is likely to be halfway between the two. Of course, this can change depending on how much interest there is in the property and how many downloads of the legal pack there have been, as we use that and the viewing days as a guide.

However, don't get put off if there have been numerous downloads of the legal pack by different solicitors. I agree it may mean lots of people are interested in purchasing and will turn up to bid, however that doesn't always happen, so make sure you turn up at the auction.

When the bidding starts, try to relax. I still get tense when I'm bidding and that's after 35 years! Always let someone else do the running in terms of the bidding. Wait until the auctioneer says two things: one is 'it's here to be sold' in other words he's telling you that it has reached its reserve price the second is when the auctioneer says, 'going once', at that point make sure you are very visible to the auctioneer and get your hand up in the air. With a bit of luck, it will dishearten the person who thought he was buying it, as you are a new fresh bidder. When bidding be decisive but don't keep waving your hand at the Auctioneer - you might end up bidding the against yourself.

I have a rule when buying at auction. I set my limit at a level where I know I can make a least 20% profit out of the deal. I then allow myself to pay another 5% above my limit. if I still don't get it, I know I've given myself every opportunity to buy. If you stick firmly to your limit, you leave thinking one last bid would've got you the property. Never ever get overexcited and bid too much for property though, as there is always another one.

Always turn up at the auction yourself. Never allow anyone else to bid on your behalf. There are lots of stories of people who have done this, and their friends have bid on the wrong lot, rang up afterwards in excitement, saying they got it for half what they thought they were going to have to pay only to find out that in fact they had bought the wrong property. Take the responsibility on yourselves.

People now bid online and also on the phone following the auction by computer at home. I always advise anyone to go in person as you never know what's quite going on otherwise.

Once the property has been knocked down to you, you'll be approached by an auction runner who'll ask you to the desk to sit down, sign the contract and pay a 10% deposit. There will also probably be a buyer's fee. Make sure you check what this is prior to the auction, and factor this cost in. So many people forget to do so.

The great thing I love about buying at auction is that when the hammer comes down on your bid, it is yours. No one can then pull out on you just before you complete, or anything silly like that, it's yours - so congratulations!

I always try to have a property in one of our auctions to sell. It's a great way of keeping the cash flow going. If you buy a property very cheaply, you can always put it in the next auction without spending any money on it and see if it sells for a quick profit.

I also love the certainty of there being no messing around with solicitors or buyers pulling out and changing their minds at the last minute. Or the solicitors disagreeing with one another or reducing the price at the last moment. It's a wonderful way of trading property and you get your money within 28-days.

Some property dealers only look in after an auction to see what hasn't sold. They then make an offer after the auction and will often sign the auction contract. However, you can stipulate that you do not wish to do this but would like to deal through your solicitor in the normal way. If you're not used to the auction method and you can persuade the auctioneer to let you do this it is a safer way of buying as it allows your solicitor time to look at all the legal paperwork.

One point to mention is that the records may show what the last bid was in the room. Do not take that as a reference as to how much you should bid. The auction is over, and the property is not sold so do not bid as much as that afterwards. Remember, you're trying to buy cheap. Don't be embarrassed to bid low. It was in the auction to be sold. When the auctioneer says, 'we had a higher bid in the room', reply 'well in that case you should have taken', it with a smile on your face. No auction house gets paid if the property is not sold, so good luck!

CHAPTER 22
RESIDENTIAL OR COMMERCIAL?

You can probably tell that I am biased towards residential property on the basis that it is probably a much safer investment than commercial property.

I'm sure we are all aware of the situation currently occurring on high streets up and down the UK. The number of shops in the UK has declined rapidly in the last 30 years. More people than ever own cars, and there has been a massive increase in out-of-town retail parks.

And even more recently, the internet has transformed shopping habits. At my own home the infamous white vans turn up on an almost daily basis, coming up my drive at great speed to deliver an item either my wife or children have purchased. I must admit I haven't succumbed to this form of shopping yet, but no doubt it is only a matter of time.

Years ago, when my father had a greengrocer's shop in Felixstowe, he had an errand boy who would deliver people's food orders by bicycle. It's amazing how even that has come full circle with top supermarket delivering your food by van all over the place. Although I can assure you that the speed the van comes down my drive, and the speed the delivery boy could reach on his bike aren't very comparable.

As the times change, so do investments. With less shops being required it's not surprising that I believe residential to be a safer bet.

The difficulty with what is considered secondary shop investment, in other words 'shops that aren't in the main high street or close by' is that it's very difficult to get quality tenants who will sign a long lease of five years or more, as there is far less demand than in years gone by.

Also, they may not have any money behind them and if they walk out, what do you do? It may not be worth pursuing, although legally you are entitled to do so.

With residential property, the trend over the last 50 years has seen residential values increase dramatically, with the odd recession in between, but they recover well. There's also a huge shortage in housing stock, which has created a huge demand for rental homes.

Recently, I tried to help a friend who purchased a very nice new office building in 1990 for £1 million. He asked me to look at it with a view to converting it to residential as he said he couldn't let it without parking. The best I could offer him was £650,000. Although obviously he's had the rent for many years on the property, the property had decreased in value by at least 35% - a trend which is diametrically opposed to the residential market.

I bought an empty shop back in 1988 and I let it for £12,000 a year as a Kebab Shop. I finally got an increase in the rent a few years ago when I managed to increase it to £15,000. Not a great increase considering I've owned it for over 30 years.

Residential or Commercial?

There are exceptions to the rule and some property developers specialise in secondary commercial property. If you get a very nice building, with parking, in a very good area I'm sure it will be let and you will be successful, but overall, I will not initially invest in commercial property.

The other reason is that it is a lot easier to borrow money on residential property than it is on commercial. With commercial property, the bank will probably only lend you the money over the term of the lease and of course as soon as the property is empty the value can plummet dramatically until the shop is re let.

Of course, you can take a bigger chance and buy a vacant shop and attempt to re let it on a long lease for a good rent. But remember, in the meantime you have empty rates to pay.

Years ago, I used to buy shops with flats above. I would sell the flat off, getting most of my money back and then let the shop, but these days so many people shop online that less shops are required especially ones outside the town centre.

Over the years councils have resisted allowing planning permission to turn shops into residential houses, although now many are allowing change of use, it has now become an undisputable fact that less shops are required.

CHAPTER 23
HOUSES OR FLATS

I have converted numerous houses, hotels and maltings into flats. I've also converted a number of other buildings into what I call vertical split houses, mainly town houses. These are sophisticated developments, and as I said earlier, I'm not expecting you to start with developments like these immediately, so what we are talking about here is whether it's best to buy houses to refurbish or whether it's best to purchase a converted flat, in both cases to either let or to sell on.

The caveat to both options is if it's very, very cheap and there aren't any problems you can't get over, then it probably doesn't matter, however there are different considerations to be made for both.

The great thing about buying a house is that you are in total control of your own destiny. if it needs decorating, you can decorate it. If it's got a crack in the wall, you can investigate this yourself and sort the problem out. Apart from building regulations and whether it's in a conservation area or not, you basically do not have to ask anybody's permission to do what you want to do.

Flats are totally different because they are sold leasehold. The reason for this is that otherwise only one flat would be responsible for the roof - the top flat! This is obviously unfair, so the whole point of being leasehold is that you are able to share the common parts of the building such as the roof, the communal hallway, windows, brickwork, external painting and so on. Each flat pays a fair share of the costs through a service charge which goes towards keeping the building in good order. I have very rarely come across a flat that is being sold freehold because of the above problems, so if you do come across one, do not buy it.

I would also like to choose this point to mention one of the most essential checks that must be made when considering a flat, the exterior cladding. The problem of combustible cladding became apparent after the tragedy at Grenfell Tower, which cost so many lives in London. Your first question when considering either a single flat, or later in your career perhaps a block of flats, should be about the safety of either yourself or those who will be living there later. If you do come across a block where there is a safety issue with the exterior cladding, ensure you do adequate research and put fire safety at the forefront.

As I mentioned before flats are leasehold, you want to make sure there is a minimum of 100 years left on the lease. That's the first thing to look at as when it gets down to 80 years a number of building societies will not lend on it. Of course, technically if the lease runs down to 0 years the property refers back to the freeholder who has retained the building as a long-term investment.

However, don't worry about that because under current law you can apply for an extension to lengthen your lease. There is a mathematical calculation that is carried out to get to a fair price for the time extension. Most chartered surveyors will be able to help and advise you on this, and if you cannot agree a figure you can go to the Land Tribunal whose final decision is binding. The freeholder cannot refuse to extend the lease. If he does, again you can go to the land tribunal where the matter will be settled at no cost to yourself.

I own a freehold in Exmouth and one of the flats only had 14-years left on the lease when the owner died. The family sold me back the lease, I think for some £30,000. I then refurbished the flat and we sold it again for £175,000 after extending the lease.

You now have far more control being a leaseholder than ever before, however make sure you look at the lease carefully as there may be restrictions. For instance, it may say you can't have pets, or you need to ask permission before you make certain décor choices. It will definitely say that you have to get permission for any structural works that are required. I can't believe how many times we get a letter from a solicitor acting for the purchaser of a leasehold flat, where we are the freehold owners, checking that the current owners have got to seek permission to do certain works and they have not.

It never ceases to amaze me how many flat owners do not seek the permission they require for making alterations to their flat. When they come to sell the flat and the solicitor acting for the purchaser asks the question, 'Have you got written permission from the freeholder to do the alterations?' They then contact us, if we are the freeholder, in a panic asking for a letter to confirm that as the freeholders we are happy with the alterations. Having not had any information about the works carried out, they then wonder why we are not happy to immediately grant them the letter they require.

In reality, they could probably go to the land tribunal and get permission to do so without any charge, however of course they have a buyer and are in a hurry to sell and will have cash proceeds from the sale to be able to pay us for giving them permission. It may sound harsh, but we always charge what we think is appropriate for the letter giving them permission retrospectively.

The next issue is the service charge, which is the cost of running the building, together with a sinking fund towards external maintenance when it's required. The sinking fund is a very important mechanism for looking after the long-term condition of a block of flats. It's basically a way of making sure that every year a percentage of the service charge is put on deposit for the large items that may need doing every five to six years, such as external redecorating. You need to be aware that any buildings over two stories high need to be have scaffolding erected which has increased the price of external decoration enormously.

Under recently introduced laws it is now possible for the residents of a block to manage it themselves. It is also possible for them to get together and purchase the freehold amongst themselves as long as you have over 50% wishing to do so.

The current freeholder cannot refuse either request. If the price cannot be agreed, again the land tribunal will step in, for which they are very much on the side of the tenant.

Personally, I think this law is unfair as I've been caught both ways, having to sell the freehold on a block of 40 flats and also lost control of the management in other blocks, even though I still owned flats in them.

If you're thinking of purchasing a purpose-built flat, obviously there are normally less problems involved and it probably won't need so much refurbishment but still most of the of aforementioned applies. So, buyer beware! Although I have purchased flats on a leasehold basis that need refurbishing, I much prefer to own the freehold for the reasons above.

CHAPTER 24
PURCHASING NEW BUILDS OFF PLAN

This is something I've done very little of over the years, as I don't believe it to be property developing at all. What you are really doing is forward guessing the price of properties in six months to a year's time when they are ready to move in to. The alternative is probably to speak to your stockbroker and gamble with the stock market going up or down in six months' time. However, I will concede that buying new builds off plan it's probably still a lot safer than gambling on the stock market. Although I can't claim to be an authority on either.

Most developers will look to shift houses and flats prior to them being built as this helps with their cash flow at the bank. An exchange of contracts with a deposit received probably allows them to re-borrow that money, although the full money will not be coming in until the property then completes.

Some developers say they are giving you up to 15% or more discount off the full market value. Some may genuinely be doing that, however it's very difficult to say what the asking prices will be in a year's time, so you don't really know, making it somewhat of a gamble.

However, what we do know is that you'll be getting a brand-new property with a 10-year guarantee on it, which should not need any maintenance carried out on it for a few years. This will be easy to borrow money against with a buy-to-let mortgage, and most importantly easy to let.

If the market continues to go up while the property is being built it will also be easy to resell. The trick is that when you agree to buy the property and exchange contracts ask your solicitor to have a clause inserted into the contract that says you can assign the contract. This means that you have the right to sell it on before you complete and are not then liable for the stamp duty.

When buying a brand-new property, I don't think it matters whether you buy houses or flats. New purpose-built flats have become far more popular than 20th century terraced houses and you'll find it a lot easier to let a new flat than an older property. Especially because as I mentioned earlier, the trends for what people want has changed, with many now wanting show-home like properties.

CHAPTER 25
TRADING IN A HOT MARKET

I use the comment that even my dog Ivy could make money in a hot rising market if she could use a paw as a signature. There is very little skill involved in jumping on the bandwagon and doing what everyone else does.

In Ireland, from 1996 through to 2007, the market kept rising very quickly and in Ireland they'd never had a proper recession in recent history.

From about 2004, on my regular trips to Aaron to go hunting, I used to say that the market was reaching its peak. I told my Irish hunting friends that they needed to get out, to which they would laugh and say here comes the negative Englishman.

In fact, the madness went further. Not only did they keep buying flats, but having bought them they would never let them, they would leave them as clean as they bought them. In other words, they didn't want them used at all, so when it came to sell them at a later date, they would still be like new. I'm sure you're thinking the same as I did, which is to leave property vacant for 23 years, with no income, sounds complete and utter madness, and it was.

One friend of mine paid €200,000 for a flat in Dublin. I was in the car when he was negotiating to sell it three-years later for €950,000. The potential buyer only offered €900,000 so he didn't take it. I couldn't believe what I was hearing. That flat was recently valued at just €180,000! This was happening all over Ireland and a lot of the stories you hear are far worse than the one I've just told you. Thankfully now the market is returning, and prices are on the way back up, partly since corporation tax in Ireland is now 12.5% which is encouraging many new companies to set up headquarters in Ireland.

A great friend of mine started out decorating houses. He did a number for me and within a few years he owned a one-million-pound country house. He had managed to do a number of risky property deals that in a hot, inflated market are possible to do. He then thought everything he touched would turn to gold. I remember him showing me that he had one million pounds in the bank. However, the recession came, and he lost everything, eventually selling his furniture to get the rental deposit together to rent a flat.

He never saw any fear in anything he did, but if you to keep taking risks - just like a very fast car driver does - eventually you will have a crash. Some people bounce back, but few in my experience learn the lesson.

I'm not saying you shouldn't invest when the market is rising because it is a great time to purchase. Also, there's nothing wrong in being brave and borrowing as much as you can on your investments to give yourself as much cash as possible to keep buying, but don't be too greedy. You are far better to get out of the market earlier than other people than to hang on and loose everything.

When I say get out of the property market, I do mean get out! Sell off at least half of your property portfolio and use the cash generated to pay off the borrowings you have on the remaining half of your portfolio which you are retaining. Pay your tax, have a great holiday, and wait while the rest get into trouble.

Property is a cyclical business. Every ten to fifteen years it comes full circle and there is then another property recession. This normally happens when the market is so inflated that first time buyers cannot purchase because they are having to borrow between four to six times their net income per annum.

Of course, there are also other causes sometimes such as a financial crisis, a general recession and very high interest rates.

If anyone tells you it's not going to happen or it could never happen again, be absolutely clear that it will happen! In my career, I have survived three property recessions so far. And most books about the 2008 recession will tell you that the experts believed that a recession could have never happened for the reasons or in the way that it did.

On top of this, you also had the buy-to-let investors buying a large amount of what used to be traditionally first-time-buyer properties. This is starting to slow due to the 3% levy put on stamp duty by the government, initially to slow down the London market but it's also had an effect across the whole country.

My message is when things sound too good to be true it's a sign that we're nearing the top of the market, so get out a year before.

CHAPTER 26
TRADING IN A DROPPING MARKET

The best advice is 'don't do any trading in a dropping market', wait until the market bounces off the floor and there are signs that things are starting to improve.

I believe I'm extremely well qualified to speak on this subject because of those property recessions I have experienced, so far with varying degrees of success, but each one being slightly different to the last.

The exciting thing about a property recession is that by the time it's over there are few people left in a position to purchase property, so if you survive, even if you haven't got as much passion as you had before it started, you'll still able to trade because the opportunities will be vast. Property prices will be low and if you take my advice, you'll be able to get back into the market before everyone else realises it is safe to do so.

One of the first signs of stability is that new car sales will pick up. Traditionally they are the first things to reduce when the economy starts to get into trouble and one of the first things to come back when it's in recovery, before property.

If, however you have stock you wish to sell, and you should need sell in a falling market, the trick is to price it cheaper than anything else like it on the market. This gives you a window of about ten weeks in which to get a buyer, by which time everyone else's values will have caught up with your price and theirs will still be on the market and vulnerable to dropping further.

Dealers that are in denial, bury their heads in the sand and don't quickly reduce their prices will eventually take less than you to get out, so be brave, don't be greedy and reduce early. If for any reason your property hasn't sold by the time the rest have caught up with you, you'll need to cut again until it is sold.

I hear so many people say that because they couldn't sell the property for what they thought it was worth or that they would only be getting their money back, or even losing a small amount, they decided to rent it out instead. If you purchased a property in order to refurbish and sell it, stick to your plan. Changing your mind and renting it is just burying your head in the sand. For starters, the market will probably continue to get worse while it's rented out, so unless you're willing to wait a number of years you won't get your money back.

Sell it for what you can get and go again. You'll get more for your money the next time around because property will have become cheaper, and you'll then have an opportunity to make more money.

It's not always possible to make a good profit out of every property transaction. Show me an experienced property developer who has never lost a penny on a property deal and I will show you a liar. The trick is to realise when there is a problem, accept you've made a mistake and not to bury your head in the sand, but to stand up to be counted. Get out of it as quick as you can. Your first offer in such an instance is probably going to be your best offer, so take it and move on.

I never worry about the mistakes I make. Firstly, there aren't too many of them! I never dwell on them and I don't worry if I've missed a deal when someone else has gone on to make a lot of money out of it. Don't lose confidence as there is always another deal!

CHAPTER 27
ACCOUNTANTS AND TAX

I haven't got too much to say on this subject, however I do know it is incredibly important to get sound sensible financial advice from a professional. And that is not me. The accountant plays an incredibly important part in what you are trying to achieve.

I was told many years ago by a very successful property dealer to never pick an accountant who drives a new car as he will get into trouble. I can see his point of view. You want your accountant to be cautious and worried about crossing the road in case he gets run over! You don't want him taking risks, in my case this means they often don't agree with my views.

He needs to be the one giving you sensible, sound and safe advice. Whether you wish to take it up or not is then up to you of course. He'll never do what you do himself and as I said, if he's willing to, you don't want him as your accountant.

An account will advise you whether to set up a property company or to trade in your sole name. There are advantages for both, including the fact that you can earn so much a year in unearned income before you pay tax.

However, you certainly don't want me giving you advice on tax, so please get hold of an accountant before you start property dealing and explain what it is you want to do. That way the two of you can

123

plan your financial affairs going forward. As I always say, 'fail to plan, plan to fail'.

CHAPTER 28
REDUCING THE AGREED PRICE

Never feel bad if you feel you have agreed to pay too much for a particular property. The most important thing is that you do not proceed with the sale at that price.

There are numerous reasons why you might have agreed to pay too much. You might have simply got carried away. It could be that the market is dropping, and you need to reassess the price you agreed. It could be that you've found things that are wrong with the property and have a very justified reason for renegotiating the price, or it could be that you're just greedy and want to make more profit. There's nothing wrong with the last reason and I'm now going to tell you a few ways of how to get the price reduced.

If it's an agent that you work with a lot or wish to strike up a good relationship with them, clearly this won't be at the best start. In this situation, as usual, do not bury your head in the sand and hope it goes away because it won't. Don't ignore the situation, face up to it and handle the fact that you want a price reduction. All you will do by not answering the phone when they are chasing you about the deal or by making your solicitor ignore his emails and phone calls, will be to make sure they never deal with you again.

The best way to deal with an agent, or people in business more generally, is to be honest. Just explain to them why you feel the price is too high. Knowing agents as I do, they are likely to work as hard as they can to save the sale and to reach a compromise between both parties. They may not like you quite as much as you thought they would, but if you can agree a compromise on the price at least they are likely to work with you again.

Sometimes however it is really best to just bite the bullet and say, 'I've made a mistake and I don't wish to buy'. Across the industry, approximately 30% of deals that are agreed by the estate agent do not reach completion, so it won't be the first time the agent has to deal with this situation or the last, whatever they may tell you.

You just need to hope that they will deal with you again. There is certainly no point in buying just to keep the agent happy. He might make a bit of a fuss and try and make you feel bad or guilty, but you must ignore it. As I said before, there's always another deal so learn from your mistakes and move on – look back on at it as a free lesson whereas it could have been an expensive mistake.

We've all agreed to pay too much for a house, got a bit overexcited and then decided we need to reduce the price. Sometimes I've left it to the last minute, sending the 10% deposit to the solicitor, asking him to send it across to the vendor's solicitor, only then to deliver the bad news, either via the agent if I'm not going to work with him again, or via my solicitor if I am going to work with him again.

Clearly you don't really want to put an agent in a very difficult position at the last minute if you already work together. However, he can always put the blame down to you as far as the vendor is concerned, while at the same time being delighted that if they do

Reducing the Agreed Price

agree to a reduction, you will pay him something for his trouble, which of course the Vendor doesn't know about.

The trick to doing this is to be absolutely adamant that you're going to walk away from the deal. Don't reduce the price to the extent that it is ridiculous. It has to be enough so that it is disappointing to them, but not so much that they will go back to square one with another buyer, when they could have your money immediately. Make it just enough that they want to still sell the property and move on and just about doable for them. If you can find out how much they owe on the property to the bank or the building society that's great because clearly if you offer too little it may not pay even the bank or building back in which case, it's never going to happen. If you can find out what they paid for it, I can also help: knowledge is power.

The other thing to remember, is that if they come back with a compromise, which is what I normally try to do if I'm in their position, don't be totally inflexible. Initially they need to think you won't compromise, but in reality, of course you're dealing and if the deal stacks up at the reduced price they are suggesting, then you must consider it even if you go back with another figure yourself. The fact they're talking to you and not blanking you is obviously the key. You clearly won't be on their Christmas card list, but I'm sure you've got plenty of friends anyway.

Over the years I've been asked many times how I live with myself for being a property developer with a reputation for being hard-nosed and business like; how do I feel when people think I'm being unfair, unreasonable and ruthless, or taking advantage of a situation. My answer is quite simple, I've got plenty friends. I sleep like a baby and I have investors and banks to satisfy, and they always send me Christmas cards!

Reducing the price at the last minute happens all the time. I would also stress, that many people purchasing a house for themselves to live in also reduce the price at the last moment. Sometimes it's because of either the survey or valuation. It has been done to me literally hundreds of times and whether such knowledge condones your actions or not is up to you to reconcile with your own moral compass.

If there's a lot of people chasing a deal, sometimes you might be better to offer more than you think it's worth in order to get a contract and to get in control of the deal. Once you've done that and undertaken your research on it, you might find there's a very plausible reason to reduce the price.

It could be an issue with the survey, or it might be that the search brings something up that you didn't know about. It might even be that you find the vendor is desperate to sell it or any host of other problems. If you can find anything to use to bring the price down, do so. Property dealing is a business, and all property developers do well to remember this.

Clearly these tactics are at the sharp end of the property industry and will not be divulged to you by any TV property presenter, but you're reading this book to find out what happens in property dealing. As I said whether you use them or not is entirely up to you.

Reducing the Agreed Price

I quite recently had a situation where I was buying a pub and a coach house to convert into houses. They are Grade II listed and the more I investigated the deal, the more complicated it emerged the conversion was. The vendor very stupidly told me that he had a tax bill to pay on January 31st and needed completion before that date.

You probably know exactly what I'm going to say now. He must've phoned me 50 times over a three-week period. On 30th January, I told him we were ready to exchange and complete immediately which is another very good tactic rather than having to wait a month to complete. The solicitors don't like it because they have to do a bit more work, but I can't help their problems. So, I thought about the number of phone calls I took off the chap and I decided I would reduce the price by one thousand pounds for each phone call, which I did. He called me every name under the sun. I told him that's absolutely fine and that I completely understood, but that if he changed his mind to let me know.

The next day at 10 o'clock, he rang me to say that I was still a bastard, but if I could complete that day, he would accept my new price. Now some of you reading this will be appalled at what I did. However, I'm thinking perhaps I was a bit soft and could have reduced it further! My advice to you is you need to toughen up. My Backer on the deal who put most of the cash in was absolutely delighted and of course he is the one I need to keep happy, not the vendor.

However rude the vendor is to you when you deliver the bad news, always keep cool. Don't fall out with him and always give him the opportunity to ring you back and agree to the new price.

CONCLUSION

If you got this far in the book, I hope that you have enjoyed reading it, and that you have managed to take something positive from it. Being involved in the property industry is a very exciting way of life. I hope I've helped you to clarify what you are interested in and what you would like to buy.

If you haven't purchased yet, but intend to do so, I hope you will take some of my ideas and thinking on board. If you've already purchased, I hope you had a good deal and that my advice might help you in renovating, letting or selling and to help you get an even better deal next time.

If you haven't decided yet whether you wish to take the plunge and enter the world of property dealing and investing, I hope I've persuaded you to do so, it's a great life, full of excitement and challenges – there's never a dull day.

Every day I wake up not knowing what might come across my desk, who will offer me a deal and whether or not I want to take it.

Tomorrow might bring me the best deal I've ever had. Today I've already had a meeting at 7 am in my local coffee shop and agreed to sell them a building I've just got planning on to convert into three houses – it's a great start to the week.